Light

James G. Piatt

ISBN-13: 978-0692615928
ISBN-10: 069261592X

Written by James G. Piatt

Published by Broken Publications
www.BrokenPublications.com

Edited & Prepared for Publication by Jennifer-Crystal Johnson
www.JenniferCrystalJohnson.com

Cover by Jennifer-Crystal Johnson
www.JenniferCrystalJohnson.com

Broken
Publications

A
Pacific Northwest
Publisher

www.BrokenPublications.com

Other Books by James G. Piatt

The Nostradamus Conspiracy, Broken Publications 2015
Ancient Rhythms, Broken Publications 2014
The Monk, Broken Publications 2013
Ideal Society, Write Words, Inc. 2013
The Silent Pond, Broken Publications 2012

All titles available on Amazon!

Table of Contents

Light | James G. Piatt

Oh, to Be Young Again

When I was a young lad,
dreaming under the cherry tree near the cottage by the fen,
I was happy without a worry,
carefree was I
as the burnt sun caressed my face,
the gentle breeze brushed my hair,
the smile upon my lips was painted
broadly. I was in the heyday of my princely realm,
the leader of pirates and mighty ships
that floated in amusement
in swirling clouds above my head.

Those golden days of yesterday are now gone,
and the cottage and fen
mere summer memories in an aging mind.
At the mercy of the fourth dimension,
my legs no longer leap from mound to mound,
no easy breath to run the youthful race.
Old memories linger in my mind
as I journey along another road less traveled,
a winter road filled with rocks, barren earth, and coldness.

Oh, to be young again and run freely
amidst flowered paths leading to new visions
in warm and verdant dells filled with songs of birds
and whistling warm winds swirling in
hot summers and lazy springs.
Carefree and without worries of adult things,
without taxing decisions and demands of labor,
I would feel a newness in all matters
and enjoy even unimportant things.

As I Remember

The tender melody from a string quartet playing Mozart
softly stirred the faded memories within my mind.
Nostalgia came flowing into my awakened soul...
the cello playing its poignant song of yesterday
painted a picture of youth dancing in the fields of delight,
arms encircling a beautiful girl with auburn tresses
and a lovely freckled face with a soft, beguiling smile.

Then distracted thoughts—
like the beating wings of a humming bird—
thrust my vague and aging mind into shadowy thoughts
as I realize that such beautiful years will now be fewer,
and a desire to control the hours of love and happiness left
bears down upon my being,
so the soft memories of past happy times
will not be clouded with dark nightmares
of our final chapters together.

Thoughts of Winter

Thoughts of winter arrived yesterday.
Fall faded and, no longer still:
The rains of winter have come to stay.

Barren vestiges of white and gray
Winds arriving cold and shrill:
Thoughts of winter arrived yesterday.

Warm thoughts have gone away,
Flowing into a tiny, frozen rill:
The rains of winter have come to stay.

The low-lying sun now has no sway;
Winter appeared with no frill:
Thoughts of winter arrived yesterday.

The dull yellow beams of the sun's ray
Now only a distant and faded thrill:

Lonely, cold memories do dismay...
Thoughts of winter arrived yesterday;
The rains of winter have come to stay.

The Coming of Winter

That time of year when warm days leave,
When clouds amass and rains appear;
These are the times when hearts often grieve,
For cold days are damp, dark, and austere.

Without the rains, however, the earth would die;
Flowers, bushes, and trees would wilt away.
Without the snow, small children would cry,
And a white Christmas would never be gay.

The rain brings a solemn troth and verdant scene;
Without winter, nothing would ever be green.
These gifts of winter one should not loathe;
Without winter rains, there could never be both:
New verdant greenery or brassy baby birds.

A Wintry Sky

I sit on a wooden bench
With my dog by my side,
Watching tiny bugs crawling
On damp earth below,
Gazing at geese flying
In a crooked V above.

I spy a small sparrow
Drinking beads of water
From a dent in a hollow stone.
A blue bird examines
A fuzzy caterpillar
With a vigilant eye.

A gentle wind quickens;
My mind hastens
To find truth hidden
Silently among drops
Of white moisture.

An Ocean's Sonnet

Open to all minds, hidden grandeur calls;
On white-topped waves atop a mist-borne night,
The ocean roars gnarled wood strewn affright.
A tiny rill crawls and a swift stream falls
Down jagged cliffs with spurts and palls;
These are alike in God's unequivocal might:
All water emulates the one infinitely bright.
The Lord made Eden open, but man made barriers;
Yet the vast, briny ocean from all sin is free,
The tide rises and green swells break.
Evil men, like burning sand, will surely bleed;
Unbridled passions flow for the devil's sake.
Such love often lays rotten like man's greed...
Then the soothing tide returns to ease man's ache.

A Sonnet to Spring

An ode to spring, the gayest of seasons, which
Brings to all a crispness of new being, and
To all who love, thousands of reasons to
Awaken in their souls' new ways of seeing:

The trees are fresh and verdant again,
Rivers slow down to a leisurely stream,
Meadow flowers begin their colorful reign,
Young hearts in love begin to dream...

The animals from hibernation arise and
Scamper to see the beauty in the leas, and
With tiny, furry feet scurry to improvise,
While tiny birds sing gaudy songs in jubilee.

Thoughts of Home

Crisp evenings,
Dark clouds, and
Winter wind
Make the
Inside of any house
The grandest of mansions:

A warm fire and
The gentle laughter
Of tiny souls
Bring the world together
After the strains of a
Tiresome day.

Happiness never strays far
From a family
Filled with love and
Caring;
It hastens its return.

Children are as fragile flowers:
When they
Are showered
With gentle drops of love,
They never wither or
Fade in beauty.

Fall's Arriving

I hear the breath
Of fall's last gasp...

In the midst of white
And chilly winds,

It coldly foretells
The final day

Of summer,
Where tiny birds

To weather bend, and
A warm dog
becomes

The hobo's
Best friend.

Childhood Memories

In the snow, a path I perceived around
An old carousel, now gone,
Tracks of a dog and child...
Was it only in my memory?

Recollections become clearer:
Home for Christmas, a
Drawer in a childhood
Desk now empty,
An old copper kettle that whistled;
A blur of past garden colors
Passed suddenly through my mind.

I felt the smoothness of stones on a path...
Rain sprinkled a flowing river,
Ripples appeared under lily pads,
Yellow flower pollen covered
Dry pine needles strewn
Loosely over faded deer trails.

I sat on a bench smoking my pipe
While my reminiscences staggered sadly past
My presence. I sighed at the ancient
Scenes as they passed by like an old movie;
Then I softly wept.

An Ebony Reality

The oaken stile, entrance
Into a rock-strewn meadow,
Leads to pine and oak trees
With leaves of ecru spikes,
Laden with thorns that bleed into
The rocky memories of my
Mind.

Songbirds singing like golden harps
Split the reality within my
Tightly woven mind into hopeful
Dreams, and harken metamorphic
Memories and tinted thoughts, which—
Like rough, chiseled visions—
Lighten my ebony reality.

Now and Then

Old woman wrapped
In wrinkled years and
Yesterday's memories
Traipses beside
Young girl wearing
Youthful rebellion and amorality,
Their steps out of synchrony;
Lives, too.

The old one lives
In bygone times;
The youthful one lives
In future fantasies.

They ramble out of pace
With time and each other,
Faltering at significant intervals
In their mutual non-awareness
Of their exclusive and separate existences:
The old woman living
Unsuccessfully in the past,
The young girl living
Unsuccessfully in the future;
Neither of them existing
In the beautiful potential
Of the ever-present now.

Motion

Life and death—
Entwined—
A symphony, finite time,
Infinity,
Inseparable pieces
Of a single reality.
Always together:
Growing, dying, being, and nonbeing;
Always apart,
Changing and unchanging.

In life,
We experience death;
In death,
We experience life.
Our bodies,
Living seeds,
Die
Then begin life anew,
Our existence a
Paradoxical quandary.

A rushing river
That overflows
Becomes a lake
Then dries up.
We, like the river,
Are the past, present, future,
We are
That which is,
That which will be, and
That which will cease to be.

We are one, yet
We are many;
We are all things and
We are no things.
We are born,
Live, die, and are reborn...
All of life is motion.

When I Am All Alone

I feel the silence, which has no sound.
It is the silence where no sound can be, not
In the caverns of a dreaming mind or
Far under the earth's deepest sea;
In the barren desert where life was once abound,
Not even Arabian whispers can be found.
All things are hushed as clouds wander free, and
Never a voice is heard above the fertile ground.
In the verdant meadow with its bushy wall
Where deer and elk once have been, cicadas
In their sixth year of sleep cannot call and
The stealthy puma listens to the wind.
Where softly flowing rills echo and mountains moan,
It is there I find silence when I am all alone.

City Dreams

Near the street where I dream,
Moreover, watch youth flit and fly
Under a silent evening sky;
Feelings from the neon lights do teem
Into my anxious mind, so unforeseen,
And into the pavement so hard and dry.
Dark clouds scud by with a single sigh and
People move swiftly as if in a dream.
My thoughts continue to wander
To and fro, from thought to thought,
Arriving upon the city street's ugly lore.
My saddening mind has but to ponder
The happy feelings that once were brought
By those peaceful images of a warm seashore!

Pain Covers My Fears

Ashen-tipped clouds slowly
Climbing,
Climbing,
Climbing
Over snow-covered,
Rocky peaks like a
Soft, furry ibex
Bounding
From crag to crag.

Deep glades,
Pockets of anguish
Hiding inside the
Snowy whiteness
Like ancient
Thoughts,
Which can only be
Reached by lonely,
Twisted patchwork
Paths
In the lobes of my
Weary brain.

Like an
Ancient quilt, they are
Woven of sorrowful
Memories,
Leading to lonely
Mountains
Where bristly brown
Pinecones—
The prickly husks

Of my consciousness—
Cover my soul and
Their barbs
Of pain
Cover
My fears.

Life

You are a jealous mistress,
Covered wordlessly
In your silken veil

You are too miserly,
Allowing too few
Years of happiness

You are too complex
For simple folk
And dreamers

You give too little,
Take too much
To partake in fullness

You are too long
For those who live
In physical or mental pain

You are too short
For those who live
In serenity and love

But what would we do
Without your boundless
Gifts of timeless possibilities?

The Stone

I have eternity in my being, but
My body is turning to sand
Under a hot August sun.
The sycamore tree is not as old
As I, but it is not turning to sawdust.
The river is much younger than
I, yet she is drying up, now just a
Lonely trickle in a stream bottom.
Who sets this all in motion?
Who allows her to dry up and
Me to turn to sand, yet saves the tree?

Where Are the Years?

I smelled of birch leaves, a
Flowing brook, small pebbles, and
Youth. My heart was composed of
Summer flowers, bumble bees, and
The scent of timelessness. My mind
Contained colorful ancient rhythms,
New poems, and thoughts of love.
These were the things strewn on
The contented paths I wandered
When I was young; in those times,
Lazy brooks were filled with tiny fish,
Colorful tree frogs, and yellow
Sycamore leaves held gaudy, singing
Insects. Those years seemed so
Abundant when I was but a youth.
Why have they now vanished... into dreams?

Another Day

The morning, crisp
As newly ironed linen,
Meets me in the warmth
Of an orange summer sun.
Long shadows cast from
The wakening sun follow
Me as I amble in the path
Of my wandering memories.
Visions of cheerful yesterdays
Arise, wrapped in tenderness.
In the sun-drenched glow
Of this summer morn, I
Revel in the fortune for
Another opportunity to
Experience one more day
In God's paradise!

Magnificent Visions

I found pleasure walking near the ocean shore,
Experienced a soft warmth below a gritty dune,
And on the yellow sand close to the ocean's roar,
I envisioned a painting where debris was strewn.

The images in the sand remain not long,
The memories in the mind also fade in time, but
The verses found in a bard's love song last
Forever in a poet's heartfelt rhyme.

Steps along life's short and complex trail
Lead to a vast array of different provisions;
They carve man's destiny upon rocks and shale,
Often giving to him magnificent visions.

Absolution

Pine needles lacing
Damp red earth,

Pinecones and berries strewn
Like brown and red jewels,

Gently covering the scarlet
Pain of past absurdities

Like the white foam of
An incoming azure tide

Covers brown kelp and
Colorful seashells,

Or like the dimness of
A holy confessional box

Covers the errors of a
Man's errant life.

Flowing

Sounds of water fleeing
Over smooth stones
Created by eons of years
In a mountain brook,

Nature's symphony shaped
By warm, gentle winds
Performing an aria through
Huge gnarled pine trees,

A ballet of oak leaves
Swaying gently,
Green clad pixies dancing
With tranquil delight!

These are the things
That flow in my
Mind, sitting by
A tranquil pond!

Days I Like

I like warm, sunny days,
Days in the vegetable garden
Planting new seeds and plants,
Days in the orchard
Sitting on a wooden bench,
Days digging slowly
In the herb garden;
I like any days around
This gentle and
Serene place where
God dwells.

Someone is Trying to Steal Your Dreams

Did someone tell you that the moon is moldy, rusty, and cold? How could that be when it is made of pure gold and can never be sold?

Did someone tell you that rainbows are not real? How can that be if leprechauns conceal the pot under an orange peel?

Did someone tell you the sky isn't there, it just looks blue? How can that be when I watch bubbles sail up into the hue?

Did someone tell you that stars will descend into the mire and everything will eventually expire? How can that be when the stars are always there for us to admire, and will continue to inspire?

Did someone tell you that some things just seem pretty and they will never last? How can that be with annual flower fields ever so vast?

Did someone tell you that butterflies are ugly maggots with wings? How can that be when they are admired by kings and queens?

Did a fairy tell you that without her no one could fly? Yet, in the heavens above one cannot deny there are thousands of airplanes to spy in the sky.

Did someone tell you we are all sinners, and that pretty girls should never kiss, and that the sun won't shine today, and it always snows in the winter, and you should never play on the beach amongst sea berries or rip tides or get sand between your toes?

Moreover, of all things, did someone tell you that chocolate and berries paint stomachs with a stain, and that the way to Never Land can only be reached through constant pain, and Peter Pan is truly dead? How can that be true when you go to sleep and see him in your head?

In addition, did someone tell you that there is no hope, and you should always wash your hands with bacterial soap, and never run at a lope? Moreover, stand at attention while on a slope and never play with a pink jump rope? Did they say that you should never dream, or try to catch rainbow trout in a moving stream, or be on a losing team, or try to write a book without a theme?

If you espy on the cliff a yellowish rose, but the wind blows it away, can it come back and be there again today? Such golden dreams shall always be like green tea and tasty brie. Life is a delicious bouquet and to do it right you have to play, and slide down slopes in a shiny red sleigh, and sing, and laugh, and dance ballet, and always have faith in each day; and never, never wear feet of clay!

Should Anyone Worry

If no enchantment is found in our poems
To entice the full moon from a far distance;
If a narcissus cannot stay the whole year round
In spite of its delightful aroma and beautiful bloom,
Should anyone worry?

If hearts like ours do not have the potency to grasp
A shining dream, nor thoughts pleasant and effortless;
If nothing can be seized for love or God,
If kisses cannot move a lover's heart,
Should anyone worry?

If the wasp should sting a blossom to death
For one drop of honey for its hive;
If the falcon should break its airy plunge—
In addition, lose its life forever while diving—
Should anyone worry?

If death is found on a shore far away from home,
Sadness clings to our hearts and passions go longing;
If the lover's moon grows fainter in the skies while soldiers
Venture from their doorsteps and never return,
Should anyone worry?

If this weary world becomes forever changed
After this decade and gets constantly grayer, colder,
Nearer to the motionlessness from whence it arrived;
If belief itself becomes paler, stiller, more bitter,
Should anyone worry?

If tears dry up and mirth becomes bizarre;
And if a soul mistrusts itself and weakens;
Since men will be men and will never change,
Moreover, because of this, will always fail,
Should anyone worry?

And if the colorful flowers become a colorless pall
Around our fresh graves when we cross over the edge;
Moreover, after we have departed, if the spark falls short
And passions devour the absurd world to its center,
Should anyone worry?

Yes.

Lonely Thoughts

Lonely memories ascend
Like sparrow hawks,
Soaring like discordant winds
Amidst tall pines in a glade,
Pouring forth murky thoughts
Which the murmurings of
My soul cannot deny.
They rise up in confusion
Atop rootless currents in the
Forlorn caverns of my essence,
Exploding into scarlet dust,
Then in the dim cell where
Sins are abolished, they
Vanish into the darkness.

Reflections While Lunching in a Garden

The old dean sat amid the early flowers of spring,
Oranges, vermilions, yellows, whites, and azure blues
All gleaming with the remnants of yesterday's drizzle;
He glanced at the cerulean sky as white clouds floated above,
Swirled and condensed in the warm afternoon sun,
Large cirrus and cumulous clouds gently hovered then hid
Over the sea green, lush mountains to the northeast.
Some still had their dark cores, but were trying to release
Moisture from the weight they carried, like men striving
To rid themselves of their dark centers of worry, pain, and fear.

A small blue bird landed nearby, one eye cocked for intruders,
The other on the water tap gently dripping life's nectar
Into a small rock basin below. Its tiny beak dipped gently into
The basin then stretched to pull the water down its throat.
The sun suddenly leapt from behind the clouds and warm beams
Streamed earthward, warming the man's weary mind and body.

His mind wandered to opportunities lost and successes gained,
Then it traveled to all the days that could have been, and
Finally, to days that would never be.
Questions, like dark umbrae, appeared and disappeared.
He realized he had had many chances, but had not taken
Many of the options offered, and in some cases, took the chance
And guessed wrongly.

He mused upon the enigma: had he lost or gained?
Only time would unfold the barren truth; the present was
Too painful to see future reality, and present reality was too
Depressing to acknowledge. Sadness crawled inside his being,
Holding hands with hopelessness.

His mind was brought back to the present as he heard voices.
People were laughing, discussing flowers, smiling contently and
Enthusiastically at the beauty that existed around them.
He realized at that moment that how one reacted at the time to
The calamities found in the world was probably far more
Important than the calamities themselves;
He realized that some minds were too sensitive to live amidst
The world's darker and more abusive side, too sensitive to
Fight back the dark-centered clouds that always hovered
Over man's destiny.
Too sensitive to make sense out of the pain and hurt
Intentionally inflicted by those who wielded power and
Malicious control over the lives of others.

The sun suddenly vanished behind the dark-centered clouds
Again. He sighed heavily as he realized lunchtime was over,
And the beauty that had surrounded him, protected him,
Thrust him into a gentler world would now disappear.
It was time to face his personal demons again, his dark-centered
Clouds, and especially his personal and malicious tormentor.
He got up from the wooden bench and left the flowers and the
Beautiful, gaudy birds behind. He shrugged sadly and left
The beautiful garden.

Some men are too gentle to live among ugliness;
It damages their souls. The old dean was one of those men.

I Am Weary

I am weary of the ugly city,
Of grimy streets and fallow days,
Of the din of commerce born of pity,
Of gaudy neon lights and nightly ways.

Let me escape to fertile woods,
To peaceful ponds and inlets blue,
To gentle winds away from 'shoulds,'
To a poet's rhyme so calm and true.

In the Meadow

Granite rocks gently whisper
Their stony poems as they
Lie basking in the heat of the sun;
They watch stoically the endless
Days that come and go,
Season after season.

Huge boulders in their lofty beds
Sit silently, staring blindly at the sky;
Stones and pebbles on the path
Grow, forming rock statues,
Idols spun of heated earth. Gray shale,
Cracked like bits of ecru dough
From the pond's dampness,
Delve into the water's depth,
Never knowing what they will find.

Bullfrogs belch their guttural songs
In unison as they stare jealously
With bulbous eyes at colored
Trout jumping to catch bugs flying by.
Together, blue birds, woodpeckers, and
Doves singing a medley of cacophonous
Notes suddenly combine in an aria of
Melodious unity.

Soft white fluffs of moisture form
Huge sculptures of mighty ships,
Stately mansions, and pirates in my
Mind. The sun reaches down
To place its balmy hand on my
Shoulders as the soft summer

Breeze caresses my face. I am
Always at peace in my private place
Of ancient paths, lazy ponds, and
Verdant meadows.

The Last Voice of Sanity

In the muted stillness
Of the broken day,
Where only silent
Memories are heard,
There resides
A hollow man
Who speaks
In hushed tones.
His voice unsteady,
Disturbed, it comes
From years inside
His head, where
Only sunbeams
Once abounded.
It is a voice that
Lacks the urbanity
Of the world;
It cries for justice
Where there
Is none, and
Peace when there
Is war... it is naïve and
Unpretentious,
Soft and mild
In its demeanor.
It is the last
Voice of sanity... yet….

I'm Going to the River... in My Mind

I plan to see the ancient, moss-covered
Boulders sitting in the lazy river, and
That old scarred rainbow trout that
I tried to catch a hundred times.

I plan to sit under a white-barked
Sycamore tree amidst colored flowers,
Soft green ferns, and granite stones, and
Allow my mind to rest under a blue sky.

I plan to write poems, listen to
Taylor, Dylan, Miles, and Ella
On the radio, and watch clouds
Languidly form into puffs above the hills.

I plan to drift back into memories of
A time when my hair was still blond,
My body firm and tan, and my mind
Able to remember names and places.

I plan to use rhymes to commemorate my
Auburn-haired love while I listen to the
Soft gurgling of an indolent stream where
Bullfrogs croak guttural love songs.

I plan to soak up the sun on my shoulders,
Breathe in the smell of the sage living in the
Cracks of the gold colored shale, and
Enjoy the beauty of a quiet meadow.

I plan to listen to blue jays and acorn
Woodpeckers squawking in the
Distance and watch sparrows jumping
From limb to limb catching butterflies.

Moreover, someday I plan to go there again
For real—just one more time—to keep memories
Of those wonderful visions fresh in my mind.

To Be With You

To be with you on this autumn day... to
Listen to brown leaves that whisper
Crackling songs of love and downy
Birds that warble poems of affection,
To observe yellow butterflies flitting
Under giant white-barked sycamore trees,
Where only a soft breeze can be felt.

When the sunlight caresses your face and
The gentle breeze combs your auburn hair,
I know I can only be in love with you and
No one else; I yearn to hold you closer as
Each new day welcomes us with a golden glow.

I promise to never depart from you and
Never leave your side; and when the din
Of humanity can no longer be heard,
Only the beat of your heart, I will embrace
You in my arms and kiss your coral lips.

Then I will take you in my arms as the
Ocean holds the current in its briny grip, as
The sky holds misty clouds in its bluish hands,
As the verdant mountains hold streams in their
Earthly grasp; I will embrace you eternally
In my heart, and my love will last forever.

Love Danced

Love danced
Gaily
In the moonlight,
Where fiery dreams
Hid in snow, whiteness
Covered sounds
Of love, and
Moonbeams
Skimmed across
Passions, covering
Longings clothed
In yesterday.

Your hair
Released aromas of love,
Of lilac scents and
Perfumed roses.
Scudding clouds
Sheltered the fever
Of my passion as
Stars reflected
The brevity of
Time left
In Prometheus'
Golden lair.
Bells pealed in
A tower, recognizing the
Finality of the
Ephemeral moment of
Our youthful love.

The Old Coyote

The old coyote howls
its eerie sound in the
dark hours of the night;
it moans its haunting notes
into my dreaming ears.

It sends forth rasping rhymes,
Evocative, unnatural sounds
of that which is frightening;
it is an unworldly, impious moaning
that sinks into the murky soil.

It is unified with all that
breathes in the darkness and
thrusts my mind into the damp
earth until it tastes humanity.

I long to see that old coyote that
howls such ghostly songs, but
it has passed unobserved into
the obscurity of its own
shadows... and mine.

Just Sitting

Just sitting on the rock-strewn
Edge of a lazy flowing stream,
Listening to the rhythm of
Guttural tree frogs that moan and
Crickets that create shrill poems on
Unearthly strings....

The golden orb beams its warmth onto
Dry earth as the wind writes rhymes
Into my soul. I yearn for my younger
Years, remembering the time loaned
To me was precious, and that which is
Left is few.

My Daughter

When upon your smile I rest my gaze,
I see truth untangled from earth's haze;
I smile and find my heart filled with glee
When beneath the blue sky I sit with thee.
The flowers do not have a sweeter scent
Than your smile which is heaven-sent;
You are my joy and my serenity when
You sit and quietly converse with me.
Your softness and beauty, too, is
A grace sublime and honest, too.
So let us sit awhile, just you and me,
Under the boughs of the apricot tree,
Listen to the breeze that sings, and
The soft murmurings of little things!

In Aphrodite's Garden

In Aphrodite's garden where love is aglow,
Among the blooming cherry and hornbeam low,
Amid the colorful flowers of passion's perfection,
Amid our shared dreams of clear introspection,
Love wandered freely under a clear blue sky.
Where hawks and sparrows fly up high, soaring
Thoughts will build rhymes which do not belie;
Soft memoirs will become my love song
        In Aphrodite's garden.
In this restful hour without the urban lie,
Among tall trees which shade the sky,
In a place where love arrives with the dawn,
We allowed our dreams to softly glow
        In Aphrodite's garden.

Nighttime

When the sun dies, the glow in the land is dead;
night arrives and the garden's ornate colors are shed.
When the flute is silent, its sweet voice sings not,
darkness arrives and no bird's songs are fraught.
When colors and songs leave with the empty sun,
that is when the hard task will come:
when heaven is mute in a starless night,
when wind has gone and there is darkness in sight,
no ornate colors and no sweet tune;
they pine for the sun, bringing colors and songs of June.

Lonely poets hidden from color and light
Write lyrics into the dark night:
Dreams scribbled on linen, pens moving into late hour
scatter soft words of a scent-laden bower.
When the golden orb arrives from the east,
their hearts gladden, free of the beast.
Like a wine goblet golden, they find they are no longer
beholden to the darkness held in their heart,
and their pens sing like a melodious lark.
What dark objects were discarded in vain?
What beautiful images in rhyme did they write without strain?
They looked before and then after,
their poet's mind found new laughter,
for the poem was full of color (not mundane),
and the flute played a melody, and the dark night did wane.

Anger

I was angry at the world; my anger
Was without end. I sensed the
World's chaos and warring trend;
I was angry at the world's strife, the
Anger seeped into my worried life.
I moistened my anger with a rigid fear;
It grew immense in the coming year.
I tried to squelch it with a happy song, and
A new path I walked along... my anger ebbed
With the sun bright. I found a serene thought
That was filled with light, the world seemed
Less dark and dire, and I buried my anger
Inside a pyre; onto my face a smile did grow.
I saw the balmy morn thaw the snow, and
Was joyful to see my anger go.

Autumn

It was a balmy fall day filled with the meadow's muted voice. The trees sat in silence, as if waiting anxiously for the freeze, which would soon turn their leaves to a burnished yellow and fling them into a deep sleep. The sun's muffled beams of warmth cast a sacred spell upon my mind, thawed my soul from the thoughts of the coming frigid chill. As gaudy birds sang near a placid brook, the voices in my mind quietly dwelled on summer memories. In my ears, the songs of downy birds delicately trilled. Holding my breath, I bathed in the strangeness of the day, and with my pulse gently beating, I held my worried thoughts far away, and took in the peculiarity of the hours that harkened in the autumn season.

Birth of a Rhyme

Fractured ecru shale reaching down into
The languid pond, like a cluttered metaphor
Reaching into the dampness of a poet's
Cluttered mind. The essence of cool water
With ripples on its skin from the soft
Breath of a fall day's balmy breeze
Reaches the shore of his mind; it
Laps at the mossy memories, reaching
Into the tangled roots of his soul like
The tangled roots of whispering elms reaching
Into the depths of the pond. Idle thoughts
In the temperate hours of the day shift
Anxiously in the lobes of his brain as
He gives painful birth to a rhyme.

My Father's Ashes

In the ancient array of gray emptiness, I gravitated to the frayed edges of the old chapel, which were like torn pieces of withered yellow paper. As I tiptoed through the dusty aromas of dead roses, I sidestepped sad, splintered memories lying upon a tattered Persian rug. I sat on an Edwardian settee covered with the gray webs of spiders long gone. As stark moonbeams transmitted a sudden loneliness through broken leaded windows, hints of lost voices echoed through the hallway over scarred wooden floors.

I fingered the flaws in the ragged flowered wallpaper and my life as I sat in muffled silence. Visions of dead flowers no longer emitting a fragrance, like long gone ancestors whose bones lie in earthen tombs no longer emit life's vibrations, covered the hallway of my past reminiscences. I noticed a tiny flower burrowed into a corner and attempted to pry it out with my pocketknife, used like a burial trowel to pull out weeds in an overgrown cemetery... and my cluttered mind. I found it had roots reaching deeply into the profusion of rotting boards, giving it life in the midst of death.

I still sensed under my fingernails, gritty ashes that I once dispensed into a hole in stony earth; I tried, but failed to touch the essence of life long gone, and the vestiges of a soul that had left. I can still visualize the short walk to the mossy stone I used as a tombstone, the soft flowing brook far below and gnarled oak trees along the way. I can still feel the balmy breeze that skimmed over my head coming down from the trail, and the din of an acorn woodpecker filling holes with acorns, like a son filling a hole with his father's ashes. It was all so fearful, yet knowing now that life is but a minuscule bit of our total existence, I no longer feared death.

I Often Wonder

I often wonder if the world gets weary
    From bombs, bullets, and angry men,

If mountains get weary
    From being alone high in the sky,

If the ocean's waves get weary
    From salt, kelp, and the waves' din,

If the deserts get weary
    From boredom of the sand so dry,

If man gets weary
    From striving for power and gold,

If politicians get weary
    From playing the fool's game,

If furniture gets weary
    From being constantly sold,

And if reality gets weary
    From trying to remain sane.

Silence *Paisible de Mes Désirs*

Blue-green waves burst
With fervent abandon
Over jagged rocks as
The turbulence of the
Sea tosses white spume
High into the air; the
Perpetual drops of brine
Upon my face dampen
My rootless senses. The
Unyielding rip currents of
The everlasting ocean slashes
At the silent screams of my longings,
Forever fleeing into scorching
Sand while the scents of the past
Roam stridently in the crevices
Of my soul. As the tide wanes,
The spirals of inexhaustible hours of
Unending motion merge into
Briny dreams, and then vanish
Into the unending voice of time.

What Would Happen?

What would happen if we forgot what war was,
And listened instead to the gentle croak of a frog
At night, when the moon was high and
We were safe in our comfortable beds?

What would happen if we forgot what hate was,
And listened instead to the soft murmur
Of ring-necked doves in the early morning
As we walked on an old gravel path?

What would happen if we forgot what death was,
And listened instead to the gentle breeze wafting
Through tall pines in the cool of the evening
While we swung happily on a wooden swing?

     We may never know.

My Son the Artist

The artist impugns
The trappings of man's
Progress because
He is able to see reality
As it truly exists.
He listens not to
The gaudy, incessant
Humming of the
Financially obsessed;
He never listens to that
Which is mundane or finite.
He listens to the infinite
Silence of the universe,
With no worldly or
Preconceived interpretations.
He invents color, form, and
Space into new meanings....
From diversity he creates a
New realism, from order
He creates chaos, and
With a swift touch of his
Brush, he creates beauty.

Weep Not, Adonis

Weep not, Adonis,
For love comes with spring.
It brings a poem to overcome
Your sadness,
It wipes away dark winter tears
From your being, and
Awakens in your heart
A sudden gladness.

In Echo's embrace, your
Happiness will climb
To higher and higher splendors
Of crimson ardor,
Expunging the dim world
Of a darkened rhyme
Under the bountiful bouquet
Of a rose-covered arbor.

Echo will break the spell
Of the darkened night, and
Enclose in your heart a
Gleaming halo at dawn.
She will bring into your
Being an impulsive delight, and
Into your soul, she will
Create a sweet song.

Don't Forget the Beauty

In our rush to gain material
Things, our souls
Get lost in the frantic pace
Of constant accumulation.

Don't forget the beauty of

A forest filled with giant red trees
That reach to the heavens, and
The lacy soft green fern beneath them;
Small, quiet blue tarns tucked
Inside verdant mountains
Surrounded by white-barked aspens
And giant sycamore trees.

Don't forget the beauty of

Small chipmunks scurrying for acorns,
Majestic hawks far above looking for prey,
Rainbow trout leaping in clear mountain streams,
Tiny pollywogs wiggling in small creeks, and
White-capped mountains of white and green,
Translucent salty blue-green ocean waves,
Multicolored wildflowers of blue, pink, and red, and
Bluebirds, robins, woodpeckers, and gray quail.

Don't forget the beauty of

Hidden glens tucked between yawning
Mountainous chasms forming deep,
Verdant, peaceful dells; white, yellow, and
Blue butterflies flitting about

In hidden groves of lush green, and
Spider webs glistening like diamonds.

Don't forget the beauty of

Small brooks with colorful wood frogs,
Lazy silver carp, and smiling, innocent children
Giggling as they play in shallow pools, and
Grandfathers wearing baseball caps and
Lopsided smiles.

Silver Tears

Silver tears run down my face
When I observe swollen dead trout
In murky, fetid ponds;
    Man's pollution brought the devastation.

Silver tears run down my face
When I observe bloated black children
In dark, foreign desert sands;
    Man's hatred produced the carnage.

Silver tears run down my face
When I observe people losing jobs
In America's main streets;
    Free markets caused the hardships.

Silver tears run down my face
When I observe families losing homes
In America's small towns;
    Bankers' greed triggered the desolation.

Silver tears run down my face
When I cannot find a hidden lair
In which to hide the
    Numbness of humanity's pain.

Silver tears run down my face,
Like broken splinters of glass
Puncturing the serenity of
    My own secret complacency!

Man's Inequities

I hear the sound of
Whales in peril; I
Smell the rotting
Bodies of beautiful
Rainbow trout in
Decaying streams; I
Watch oceans turning
Dark with the sludge of
Ugly cities' sewer
Drains;
I hear forests smoldering
In the fires of greed;
I smell the yellow
Air, and watch the gray
Sky filled with particles
Streaming from smoke
Stacks covering the
Once verdant meadows;
I hear, smell, and
Watch as the earth
Gasps in the aftermath
Of man's inequities...
Then, feeling impotent,
I weep.

Joyful Rhythms in My Mind

Teal colored waves bursting over mossy rocks,
The never-ending sea tossing white, foamed, sweet
Moisture high into the air; fleeting drops of brine
Upon my face awaken my drifting senses.

The eternal tide of the ocean softly
Carries the whisperings of that which is pleasant
Into the smooth, hot sand. Visions of things which
Are beautiful stream quietly into my soul.

As the peaceful day ends and the ocean's current
Ebbs, blue-green sprays of sweet moisture
From the sea's abundant source wash
Salty dreams into my being, which vanish
Into the joyful rhythms of my mind.

When I Breathe

When I breathe,
I find my
Breath is
A magenta-tinted
Mist in
The twilight
Of the evening. I
Try to crush
The silent peal of
The grumbling
Of passing days
Under my feet.
I fail to recognize the
Fact that, although
Man constantly changes,
Time never does.
The sun arrives and
The moon disappears, and
The earth miraculously
Still exists every
Single morning...
In spite of man.

I Dreamt

In the crimson haze of an unexpected day,
I dreamt of things I recalled along the way.
Pink iris and red roses on perfumed paper;
Scents of rust and smells of misty vapor.
I listened to the sun as it slid into the air and
Dreamt of ceramic gnomes that sit and stare,
Of humpback whales and warty toads,
Of gravel paths and wandering roads.
I dreamt of times when life was gay,
Of special conversations of the day,
Of silent ponds and verdant trails,
Of rhythmic poems and magic tales.
I dreamt of places near and far,
Of rumbling waves and a shooting star,
Of times when I was not so gray,
Of balmy winds on a summer day, and...
I dreamt of times when we were together,
Of happy picnics in the warm weather,
Of gazing at bright stars at evening time.

Twilight Time

In the twilight minutes of the day's end,
When the sun's rays no longer bend,
The soundless shadows of the trees
Hide beneath the curling breeze...
My evening dreams start to wander
As I sit in silence, taking time to ponder.

The daylight hours will soon die
Under the clouds in a fair night's sky;
It will be time for warty frogs to sing with
Their baritone and deep bass ring;
The dove's final cooing will start to fade.
I will then listen to An Ode to the Piano, so dear,
As the moon comes and offers me good cheer.

Waiting For....

Summer, fall, winter, and spring
Scratching at our memories,
Tugging at our minds, creating nostalgia:
Lost toys, misplaced relics, broken seashells,
Christmas presents, birthday cakes, Easter
Eggs, weddings, pictures in albums, vacations
At the beach, rivers, parks, and lakes…
Children being born, children having children,
Graduations, jobs, special dinners, coming home,
Going away, health, sickness….
Things vanishing so quickly in the twinkling of time's eye:
So many years of memories in boxes of saved things,
Poems un-written, stories half-forgotten, songs still
Lingering, lingering, lingering in our fading
Minds... waiting for....

Sounds of Hope

Loneliness leaves as thoughts ascend
Like sparrow hawks into the sky,
Soaring like strident winds
From tall oaks in a glade,
Pouring forth memories
Which the murmuring of
Longing souls cannot deny.
They increase in riotous turmoil
Atop wandering currents of
Time in the forlorn caverns
Of hopefulness, eventually
Exploding into golden dust.
Despair destroys happiness
Without compassion, therefore
Listen not to the lonely
Cries of anguish exploding like
Splintered glass, causing
Silver hollowed tears to fall
Like dead leaves in a forest;
Heed only the sounds of hope
That create a peaceful
Stillness in your aching
Soul.

The Final Hour

When the final curtain is drawn and
The hours of life unfold, we breathe our
Final breath, so long, and wait for
Heaven tinted in gold. The things
Savored in this life—loving mate and
Children glad—these memories fade
With death's dark song, and remaining
Hours become lonely and sad. As
Light dips into the endless fire and
The gentle time on earth is gone, the
Orbiting sphere sings its final dearth and
Soon the reflexes known as life expire,
As does an existence that held such worth.... But
God's tenderness comforts the final hour.

The Sky's Painted Skin

The sky's painted skin,
The metaphor of my hidden thoughts,
Echoes a melancholy in my soul.

As I mull over my thoughts, I long for
A love song and a poem of serenity.

I seek out answers from the glimmering neon lights born in an
ugly city, and in the darkness of alleys I search for solutions; I
follow nightmares into the obscurity beyond the security of my
mind and find only darkness.

Even where precious feelings once shimmered in a golden hue, I
find lifeless stones of sorrow.

Only amid the fading glances of special memories where my soul
restrains the murky vibrations in my brain; moreover, only when
there is no worldly intrusion do I find harmonious tranquility!

All Sad Memories Faded Away

All sad memories faded away...
My mind is now silent, calm, and still;
They eschew the clarity of a bright day.

In colorful glass the shade of whey,
Peaceful echoes reverberate upon the hill;
All gloomy memories faded away.

In the sunbeams of the coming day,
They will hide behind a soundless rill;
They eschew the clarity of a bright day.

Darker thoughts were quickly swept away
From around the window's ancient sill;
All gloomy memories faded away.

And in the serenity of Tao's way,
With luck, we will break the devil's will;
They eschew the clarity of a bright day.

In the aroma of a plaintive bouquet,
In our minds open to all goodwill,
All dark memories faded away;
They eschew the clarity of a bright day.

Teach Me

Teach me

The mermaid's song, to understand
The laughter of a child, and decode
The Zephyr's messages...

Teach me

The sun's heated voice, the
Moon's cool rhythms, and the
Stars' distant messages...

Teach me

To savor the herb's spicy
Tang, the sweet taste of
Cool water after a long trek...

Teach me

The soothing grace of a
Soft pillow at night, the
Orange dawn when I arise...

Teach me

How to remember the sound
Of honest laughter, moreover,
Forget the voices of avarice...

Teach me

The beauty of colorful flowers
And the mightiness of towering pines...

Teach me

To love the unlovable and
Care for those in need...

Teach me

The essence of the silent poem,
The still pond, the whistling of
Birch trees bending in the wind...

Teach me

To grasp the rumbling sound
Of waterfalls and the soft
Murmuring of the dark soil...

Teach me

To remember the rhythm
Of peaceful times and
Forget the tempo of bloody wars...

Teach me

The cadence of our short life, and
To appreciate calm and quiet days...

Teach me

To savor each hour and
Have dignity among the
Undignified...

Teach me

To bend when I wish
To stand rigid, and to listen
To those of contrary hearts...

Teach me

To hear choirs of angels and
The roaring voice of an
Ocean's rushing tide...

Teach me

Not to wallow in my own
Misfortunes, but help me
To give solace to those
Who are unhappy...

Teach me

To be that which I can be and
Forgo that which I cannot,
To accept success with humility and
Failure with elegance...

Teach me

To take the road less traveled, and
Not the treacherous path of pride...

Teach me

To love the truth and shun
That which is not, embrace
Righteous souls and avoid
False minds...

Teach me

To comprehend the artist's mind,
The poet's soul, and the writer's
Skill...

Teach me

To desire fewer things,
Be satisfied with less, and
Enjoy simple Wednesdays...

Teach me

The way to create serenity
In a world filled with the din
Of terror...

Teach me

Not to fear the darkness of the
Tomb or the crackling of
Aging bones...

Teach me

How to take Your hand and
Listen closely to Your voice.

Summer Time

Silver, soundless,
My soul's memories
Rise up in hope
Like the blue-green
Rapids of a slow-
Moving stream,
Like a downy dove
Atop currents of a
Warm spring breeze.
Delicate, fluttering leaves
Gleaming on sycamore trees
Calm my anxious thoughts;
Nature's warming symphony
Sings in my longing soul as
Verdant reeds with
Furry brown tops
Sway in a balmy wind.
The wrinkled skin
Of a lazy pond ripples
In glee as my
Troubled thoughts
Are covered
With contented illusions,
Scattering my fears afar.

I Keep Walking

Dead trees
On the edge
Of a crystal brook
Bend to the breeze
Like a restless crowd
Awaiting the subway.

I watch in silence,
Feeling an uneasy
Disturbance.
I stand erect,
Straighten my shoulders, and
Fearfully hum a song
Of the past.

I turn and quickly
Walk away,
Having
No place important to go.
Having
Nothing important
To accomplish,
I smile and just keep walking.

Visions

The visions of a lea, glade, and rill,
Even the verdant earth standing still;

Hidden are the murmurings of news raw,
Hidden in dark dreams resting in straw.

After extended and soothing nights,
I envision the loveliness of passing sights...

I smell the lovely aroma pink lilacs bring
As they sit nearby a softly flowing stream.

I see mighty spires and hear holy bells
Bringing splendor into life's empty wells.

The rains arrive and then the rains go,
As do the rainbows and the snow.

The stars, sitting like sentinels tight,
Silently guard the moon at night.

The sunshine of mid-days conceal
The rawness of troubles seemingly real.

Birds sing joyous songs to melt all sins;
Precious brown sparrows and tiny wrens.

Let life be gay, let children merrily scream,
Let mothers of happiness always dream.

Sing uplifting songs to let the earth heal
From crimson wounds of war so real.

Winter is Here to Stay

Sweet visions of warm winds are fading away,
The ocean's tide no longer calm or still;
The icy breath of winter is here to stay.

Frozen streams and barren trees dismay,
My summer heart is abandoned and shrill;
Sweet visions of warm winds are fading away.

Cold thoughts linger as sunny dreams decay,
The mountains are white with winter's chill;
The icy breath of winter is here to stay.

The unfriendly winds blow icy and gray,
Turning the sun to the iceman's will;
Sweet visions of warm winds are fading away.

Unfriendly gusts of winter are due again today,
Blowing warm thoughts away from the hill;
The icy breath of winter is here to stay.

In the months ahead, the cold wind will go away;
Sunnier days will reflect upon a rill, but for now
Sweet visions of warm winds are fading away, and
The icy breath of winter is here to stay.

In a Garden

In a garden where birds soar slow
Among the oaks and sycamores low,
In the soft, warm soil of God's perfection,
Amid the streams of circumspection,
My mind wanders freely under a clear blue sky.

Where wrens and sparrows softly fly,
My thoughts build a poem that will not belie,
Soft memoirs soon will become confection,
In a garden where birds soar slow.

A restful time without urban duress,
Among the trees with shady excess,
A peaceful day listing to a dove
With its soft cooing and words of love...
This place is a sign to all above and
Hope to all of those on this plateau,
In a garden where birds soar slow.

Special Times

During special times, love doth grow
Among green wreaths with the holly bow,
In the long year of changing inflection,
Amid the striving against life's imperfection,
Love continues to develop, calmly... slow.

Like colored lights, bright dreams radiantly glow;
Love becomes sweeter like an aged Boudreaux;
Happy new memories become sugared confection
In love's sweetness during special times.

A kiss and shared caress so slow,
Lovingly shared in our white chateau;
Soft touches and words of warm affection
Are the dreams borne of introspection, and
A fitting counsel to all lovers... even nouveau
In love's sweetness during special times.

Help Me

Help me to understand

The splendor of silence,
The aroma of happiness,
The joy of solitude,
The reason for sadness,
The depth of love,
The serenity of a brook,
The hopefulness of tomorrow,
The radiance of a red rose,
The clarity of truth,
The humility of a nun,
The piety of a priest,
The honesty of a child,
The power of the ocean,
The beauty of honesty,
The meaning of dreams, and
The luxury of aging well;
For in the knowledge of
These things, I will be
Able to unearth the obscure
Passageway to happiness....

A Voice

When I was young, a voice talked to me from the depths of the briny sea, from the moisture in diaphanous clouds floating in the sky, and from the dark, damp earth taken from hollow caves. The voice was that from the past and the future, of things spoken and unspoken. It emanated from an altar covered with candles and ash, a place where white roses spewed their sweet bouquet into weary minds. I listened with fear and love, but my feet were embedded in the dark loam where low things crawl and lie, where lovers live and die. I felt the essence within the sun's beams as they caressed my being in the careless wind that carried the voice's lovely song, and in the beautiful rhyme which touched my soul. I believed that which I heard in the depth of my wondering brain, in the sinews of the muscles which carried me toward the voice, but I was young and not ready. Now that I am old and my hair is gray, my body is tired and my mind is weary, I understand the voice that I heard that day, and I am ready to go to that place, where the sun is always in the sky and where I can never again die.

A Childhood Place

There is a pleasurable place deep inside
my being, where childhood memories lie
asleep, a place where seasons are
extended and filled with long-lasting,
pleasant hours. The hills in the distance,
now green, breathing spring into my
eyes form a new place where these
present and past memories collide.

I amble in flower-lined paths once
familiar, where old faces smiled and
they, now gone, walked in harmony.
Return to me, oh beautiful places that
have vanished into dreams; bathe me
with your warmth, lovely sun, so the
childish mind of my youth can blossom
again and reveal all the sweet hours of
the past. Come back to me, special images of
youth; come back, scenes when my
heart had cheerful wings and birds sang
joyful songs. Hearken to my plea... don't
escape into the darkness of night; don't
take away the glint of youth that I feel in
my aging soul.

Country Road

Rows of corn fading into the raspberry
Dusk, green epitaphs to tired farmers of
The dark earth, holy stalks guarded by
Enigmatic scarecrows of ambiguous
Character, staring with button eyes at
The blackness of the sky filled with
Famished crows.

A mud rutted road vanishing into the
Horizon, miles of flatness… leading to an
Obscurity of monotony, ending in a
Cacophony of unbroken silence where
Two elderly folks happily watch old movies
On an antique VCR attached to an
Ancient RCA television set.

The Unwritten Song

The eternal thunderous tide carries white crested waves on its surging back, tossing them with impulsive abandon onto heated sand, lining the shore with ocean creatures for the pleasure of capricious children and elderly dreamers.

The ocean's immensity covers the shoreline with rhymes of moisture as its waves arrive on the feet of a roaring mist, enveloping the shore. Sirens far out in the deep sing to those with naïve souls, using whispers to gently uncover their memories.

The fading sun leaves an orange hue on the salty steps of a summer afternoon. Tedious would be the world without the undulating tide that brings rhymes of roaring harmony into our souls as we stroll upon the hot, motionless sand. The inward bound rippling tide covers our footsteps like an unwritten poem that still exists in a poet's dreaming mind.

Daffodils

I was walking quietly as a deer,
Silently tiptoeing over a hill when
I saw a field of yellow daffodils near
A flowing rill; they were slowly
Dancing in the gentle breeze
Next to granite boulders and a
Column of white-barked trees.
The flowers were plentiful like
Stones in a lea, which form
Stony edges for paths along the
Way. I basked amid their
Companion and beauty, while
They emitted beautiful fragrances
As if it was their duty.

A Red Rose

In the shadows of a vanishing moon
In the late hours, a poet takes his pen,
Writes courageous lyrics about unselfish men,
Brave soldiers who died on this day in June.
They forfeited their lives one hot afternoon
Behind boulders and scree in a bloody glen,
So we at home would remain free again,
Not perish as they… much too soon.
Give us courage and give us power
To live justly and with grace while
Granting us virtuous minds this hour,
To grasp the reasons behind war's chase;
Grant us also the desire to plant a flower,
A beautiful red rose on a white bower.

Little Colorful Gargoyles

Tree frogs in the glare of the sunlight stare at
me with bulbous eyes, tiny gargoyles savoring
tasty bugs on sycamore leaves, looking
like gaudy clowns. They remind me of my
childhood when I used to collect them in a jar
to take home to my hand-dug pond in the
backyard of my home. They were brought in
to keep my goldfish company, which I caught
in the murky pond in the park. I used to sit for
hours watching the tiny frogs leaping from the
water flowers I planted to snag bugs flying by.
I used to dream and paint hopeful images in
the sky while watching the hours float carelessly
by. Now I am older and I wish I could gather
those hours and fill a pond with them to keep
the frogs and goldfish company... along with
my other fading dreams.

My Grandfather

It was oatmeal and cornmeal muffins with honey for dinner…
once again, Grandfather was saving the fried chicken for
tomorrow night. I didn't mind the oatmeal with cream and honey,
but to this day, I still don't like cornmeal in anything. I never
slept much at night when I stayed overnight; Grandfather's clock
clanged each half and full hour throughout the night. I usually
heard each gong until it was after three o'clock in the morning. I
could hear my grandfather snore most of the night, too, shaking
the plates and cups on the small, scarred kitchen table, but
eventually I got used to that, too. The couch I slept on was lumpy
and Grandfather's hovel was cold and drafty. Even with a heavy
wool Army blanket, I felt the chill of the incoming fog. In spite
of the cornmeal muffins, snoring, cold, and clanging clock, I
wouldn't have traded sleeping over with my quaint Grandfather
for anything.

His bedroom was gaudy with vividly colored religious shawls
hanging on the walls. I learned many years later that a huge silk
horoscope hung on the wall back of his bed. It always intrigued
me to no end. Grandfather was an intenerate Pentecostal healing
minister, a fact which I didn't understand at the time... probably
still don't.

The Mexican women in the neighborhood always loved him,
with his old-fashioned pinstriped dark blue suit (his only one),
his pocket watch tucked into a small pocket, hanging from a fob,
and his high-top soft leather shoes which he laced up with an
ivory lacer. He never worked, unless you could consider
preaching for free work, but he always said God would provide,
and it seems he was right, for he always had a place to stay, albeit
lacking in most amenities, and his Mexican women always had
meals and often a pie or cake for him, especially when I visited

him on special days. Those were exceptional times and I still miss seeing him, but I am reminded of him every time I hear his clock, which is now sitting on the fireplace mantle in my living room and chimes every half and full hour throughout the day and night.

Fall Memories

Leaves resting on the grass, wrinkled
and brown like my grandfather's old jacket,
which, he wore when he chopped
wood in the fall for the coming winter.
The grape leaves weathered, yellow,
and wrinkled, like his hands, which
pulled the clumps of grapes from their
living stems.

The mountains barren and stark,
peeking through thin clouds, the air
cold and crisp like a ceramic urn where
his ashes lie, final remnants of a hard,
full life. I am inside the old farmhouse
near a warm fire, thinking of the passage
of time and long past fall memories.

Time for Autumn

At this time when my mind is calm and
Vague dreams have passed me by,
Near a place where, without a qualm,
Pleasant memories never seem to die....
Giant gossamer clouds move silently,
Streams flow gently down a verdant hill,
Pairs of brown-tailed hawks soar quietly,
But I hear the calling of their voices shrill.
I marvel at the colorful flowers in the leas,
Listen to lovely songs of tiny birds soften
And the guttural voice of a frog that says,
"I know now that it is time for autumn."

The Doll

It is in an old sawmill where
wooden pegs that will attach
doll legs and arms to doll bodies
are first created from logs.
Small pieces of wood are then
made into small, round dowels
on an old lathe, which grinds and
screams in a soprano voice with
an inadvertent grimace of imaginary
pain. Sawdust, the minute remains
of the internal thoughts of the once
majestic tree, fall upon the wooden
floor only to be swept away with
careless abandon at the end of the day.
The dolls, made from the symphonies
of the whirling saw and grinding lathe
sleep in their crystal minutes without
knowledge of their beginnings. A small
girl, also unaware of the tree that gave
life to her doll, is tucked into her bed to
the tick-tocking of an ancient clock while
blue birds, colorful snow globes, and
lightning bugs in a jar of happy moments
float above in the smiles of her dreams.

Vanishing Hours

In the gray, fading hours of my vision, trees in the apple orchard are spinning like dark red ribbons, the meadows below the ecru hills are whirling into a shadowy golden hue; memories are vanishing into the shadows of a shade of obviate obscurity. I smell the sere earth, no longer damp and life-giving, now merely russet-colored dust and strangeness. I watch the slow whisperings of lost moments falling into the heat of the summer sun. I think of childhood things, of special moments surrounding me, breathing slowly with long sighs of a special calm.

A Day at the Shore

The tide drudging into the ecru sand, foam, and blueness rearranges the scope of reality. Tearing into the continuum of time, it causes a rift in the recurring landscape. Seashells, abandoned homes of ancient creatures, tumble onto the shore, painting pictures resembling Equuleus with its fading stars.

A tree-lined sand path vanishing into dreams carries briny thoughts to a place too constant for emotions, too harmonious for unpleasant hours. The breeze trips against ethereal and fertile memories and dissipates into bells and mantras of the language of happiness. It brings in the realm of that which is simple, and the kingdom of unhampered pleasure.

Sea grass and kelp plummet onto the shoreline, teasing gulls and terns with tiny creatures inside their being, tasty morsels like souvlaki to their eyes. Trinkets, colorful bits of glass, trickle onto the sand, breaking the ecru dullness; memories lodged inside my mind, once hidden, spring into existence with the pinkness of the fading sun.

The ocean fills with fog, drinking it into its moist body, the late afternoon arrives, and the sun sinks into the far side of cobalt vastness; the bright day borrowed from time begins to vanish and the day filled with a rustling breeze partakes in greeting the evening.

Nature's Home

Upon this summer of unspoken thought,
I recalled balmy days and a cheerful song,
Smiled at the silly things that I had once sought,
The conclusions that I had hastily drawn.
I read heartily poems of Keats and Thoreau,
Listened to the songs of Dylan and Waters,
Enjoyed a fine sip of a beautiful, aged Merlot,
Thought about wars and political squatters.
I sat by the gentle river penning a new poem,
Recalling the things I had seen and known,
The sounds of frogs croaking in a stream
Of golden fairies and a green-clad gnome;
I found things peaceful as if in a dream,
Felt safe and content in nature's home.

In the Wee Hours

In the wee hours of the morning,
as the stars shine brightly in the
heavens, I listen to the notes of
Miles Davis. His trumpet's voice
reaches into my soul and the
silence of the night embeds his
chords into the purple minutes of
my life. It is in these quiet times in
the wee hours of the morning that
my world is calm and at peace.

After the Spring Gales

After the spring gales
Arrive, after the prevailing
Winds subside, downy
Ashen clouds scudding
Noiselessly with soaking
Responsibilities drop their
Burdensome weight in lush
Pastures far below.

Storm tossed seeds rooted
In the damp earth begin to
Grow under the plentiful sun.
Yellow and brilliant,
The sun's rays topple from
The heavens, leaving a
Soft, warm blanket on the
Earth, laying down the
Platform for the entrance
Of multi-colored flowers
And peaceful summer hours.

Spring is Here

Spring arrived; it's no longer cold.
Velvety birds sing at their will;
The bright sun melted winter's robe.

In verdant meadows no longer gold,
Dappled frogs are croaking shrill:
Spring arrived; it's no longer cold.

Spring gave colors to behold,
Rills flow in chasms down the hill;
The bright sun melted winter's robe.

I longed for spring to unfold,
Watched flowers near a flowing rill:
Spring arrived; it's no longer cold.

I love beauty in flowers that unfold
As the day's warmth removes the chill:
The bright sun melted winter's robe.

After spring, summer is foretold,
To the warmth of the sun I thrill!
Spring arrived; it's no longer cold,
The sun bright melted winter's robe.

Change

The icy bands of dark moisture covering the beams from the kiln of heaven freeze unknowable possibilities in my mind. I observe, in the pallid grayness of the afternoon, the birth of illogicalities in frozen metaphors eddying across my soul.

As cold, ashen clouds fade, they abandon their obscure quest for all that which is achievable. Then the heat of the atomic furnace, which obliterates the tumultuous memories from my neurons, melts the misgivings of my stolen thoughts.

As I watch newly baked visions appear over the church's steeple in the form of brilliant egrets wading in melting snowflakes, my mind transforms the enigmas of the unpleasant paradoxes in my world.

Like an earthen bridge that spans the impossible divides of rushing contradictions, the inner transformations of my soul are carried safely to the other side. Abandoned hopes, like shards of brown clay, are crafted into new vessels.

I look into the mirror of my life, breathe a life-giving sigh at the translucent pottery emerging from the oven of creative alteration, and begin a bright new day, which is now braided with streams of expectations.

Another Time... Another Place?

Oh dark, offending scent of death
Hovering over the blackened oak
Tombs of friends and foes, when will your
Strident voice become silent so I can hear
The lone, sweet voice of a single white rose
Clinging to a faded arbor? I long to hear
Melodies so pleasant, so sweet that
I can no longer hear the distorted voices of
Angry men proposing yet another war,
Nor envision sobbing eyes of shattered mothers,
Or countless bodies of soldiers strewn carelessly
Upon an alien sand, or sad children starving
At their mother's breast. Oh, for a peaceful
Time to spend bent upon a book under a
Sycamore tree with small, smooth stones
Under my bare feet and the gurgling laughter
Of a softly flowing brook laced with granite
Boulders reaching uneasily for the sky....
Like my worrying soul, I sense the pulling of
Long past memories in my weary mind,
Feel a subtle nostalgia forming in my soul. I try to
Visualize a time when the world was not at war,
A time when we were at peace with ourselves
And others, a time and place when the pipes played
A happy tune. However, that was a long,
Long time ago... perhaps another place... or
Did it ever exist at all?

Meditating on Life

It was one of those cool spring days; the flowing stream was crinkled like old parchment as it flowed quickly toward the placid lake far down the meandering path of liquid. The tepid air motionless and tranquil, not a leaf stirred on the willow trees... it was as if he were in another place, another time... not of this world, not the world in which everyone else existed.

He was a solitary man, a man of philosophical thoughts and, frequently, melancholy. The silence of the atmosphere both calmed and terrified him. His thoughts meandered back in time over his life; it was often like this fast flowing stream, raucous and tumultuous. At other times it was a placid pond, serene and peaceful. He peeked through the veils of time at the memories hidden in the vagueness of his aging mind. He recalled the happiness and the sadness, the excitement and the ennui. He sighed and looked up to the hazy gray clouds in the sky.

The sun appeared unexpectedly and rays beamed down and clothed his body with warmth. The clouds, once gray and ominous, were now a luminescent grayish-white, a vivid blue sky framing the background. His aged skin felt the sun and he smiled. The shady memories he had experienced in the overcast morning vanished and he was alive in the present once again. He heard the soft murmuring of tiny flies as they danced around his head; he felt the temperate breeze upon his face, soft and gentle. Tiny leaves from trees along the side of the flowing stream moved ever so gently, as if a fairy had wafted a magic breath upon them.

He heard the lonely drone of a plane in the far distance and his wandering mind awoke. He gazed at the ecru shale outcropping creeping slowly up the side of the flowing stream. He noticed that many of the tree's leaves were now sprouting with a verdant newness. He knew that misty days like this would soon disappear, and eventually—inevitably—the sun's rays would bounce off the earth and the warmth of the days would increase. Soon after the winds and rains of spring, the days would get warmer and brighter. Lent and Easter would end and another summer season would slowly begin anew. It was all so predictable, so constant, like life and death.

Tomorrow would be another day, and soft breezes would carry a gentle rain impetuously over the hills, enveloping them with moisture. He wondered if he would be here the coming summer, when the sun's warmth would cover this silent place and a placid pond would subsist where the swift flowing stream now existed. He wondered if he would be able to hike along the unhurried deer path to this wonderful, extraordinarily serene place. He wondered if he would still be able to sit under the large sycamore tree amid granite rocks and boulders, basking contentedly in the heat of the summer sun. Such are the meandering thoughts of an old man whose life span was slowly dwindling into the past, and whose body was feeling the pain of many years. Such are the thoughts of all those who think deeply about the wonders of life and who have come to few conclusions, but at times feared the dwindling time as they aged, seemingly so quickly.

What are the reasons for man to exist? One's life, so temporary, so transient, so improbably incongruous. Life, a jealous harlequin prancing to and fro with lighthearted abandon, with no thought of anything but the present. Death arrives so quickly and everything that was loaned in life is taken back and given to others. What is man's purpose on this lonely piece of sod; what is his real reason to be? Perhaps in death there is an answer, or perhaps there will only be a dark nothingness. What would that knowledge mean to a person, if he or she knew ahead of time? Would behaviors be changed, would life be altered, or would it carry on much the same as it does now? It is all quite a paradoxical enigma.

The old man sighed, stretched, and gathered his gear together for the long trek back to his car. He would then drive back to his warm, comfortable home and loving wife. He was still wondering about life, after all these years. He was very thankful for all of it, and hopeful for more of it, especially more time to experience its wonders, beauty, and ponder on its meaning.

A Sense of Spring

Sounds of thunder rumble faintly behind darkened hills in the far distance. White clouds with shadowy edges gently reach down and touch the earth with moisture as a balmy wind appears, pushing away the clouds, and the sun emerges, shining on new growth in the garden. My mind slips away from its wintry mood and warm memories of past springs sweep through me; I watch the emerging colors in the garden dance to an ancient rhythm, and the essence of spring creates a feeling of newness, offers a colorful and verdant scene of beauty to behold.

A Song of Spring

A soft, balmy breeze, the breath of spring's soul,
Brings multicolored beauty to the garden's bed.
A warm, silent presence makes my heart whole
As I smell the aromatic bouquet of roses red.
Tall hollyhocks reach up to heaven's deep blue,
The geranium's pink emits waves of color bright;
Twining bluebells sing a melody of beauty so true,
Combining with hues of coral berry punch so right.
As the pomegranate sun sinks into the hills afar,
Sweet voices of songbirds echo in tall sycamore trees.
The foothills become yellow as the morning star, while
My mind is soothed by the humming of honeybees.

The Orchard Garden

Ask me not what spring brings to wistful eyes in the orchard garden; it is vibrant roses of ornate colors, pansies pink and red, and gentle blues and pinks of Irises. It is the bright yellow of daffodils and the golden glow of black-eyed Susans. It is the vibrant greens of new plants, sweet bell peppers, lettuce, cucumbers, onions, and summer squash, and the reds of tomatoes, all starting a new life in beds of lush and yielding soil.

Ask me not if you can wander on the rock-lined paths and redwood chips among the apricot, apple, and plum trees, for they are free to all to walk upon. These are but a portion of the loveliness that one can view in my garden of plentiful delights. The other portion is that of solitude of the moment, which reigns in this serene place where verdant mountains loom high to the east under white clouds of moisture.

Hours That Guide the Day

A tear has fallen softly
From a flower on the arbor,
A beautiful crimson rose
Clinging to memories that I harbor.

Dry lemon balm and chocolate
Mint are weeping in dry loam,
Aromatic scents long gone that
Covered the garden at our home.

The sweet bouquet of roses and
Herbs have also faded away... the
Garden is empty now as are the
Final hours that guide the day.

The Owl

Oh, noble owl; esteemed phantom of the darkness and watcher of obscure shadows in the night, use your large yellow eyes to see that which is unseen, sense that which stalks hidden in the shadows. Your lonely, piercing shrieks in the night worry the voles searching for midnight snacks and roil the calm air with an eerie disturbance. You splendid beast of feathered woe perching in your throne of parched leaves, heed not the call of the stars that beckon you to their ethereal flames; listen only to the damp earth as it baptizes you with its abundant prey so you may gain strength to light the lantern of harmony. Hush the night with your low, thunderous voice of peace, and squelch the weeping wail of sad hearts that are lost in the moonless night.

Time

Time, why am I so anxious as I watch you pass by so quickly, you and your mysterious shadows of the vanishing past.... You have countless hours to spare and I, of mortal clay, have so few.

The conscious pilgrimage of life ends in the scarlet seconds of wordless flight, while you continue forever. When the ocean's waves of ephemeral moments pass over our graves of earth and wood, our lifeless flesh remembers not, but you remain for those with life who still dream of golden possibilities.

As countless seasons come and go and the green grass turns brown and green again, and precious hours have long departed this life of mine, I will be visited as luminescent clouds wander freely over my cement tombstone, and someone I loved and still loves me will place scented roses on my grave.

Life Begins Again

As my mind submerges into the depths of the sea of watery dreams, filled with the calmness of chiming bells and swaying altars, I escape from worldly anxieties. There appears a delicate omen of hope in the grayish pink of slumber; in it is a panorama of meandering feelings caused by an expanding peacefulness in my soul. From the depths of dreams, I gather the echoes of joyful visions and place them inside my brain's trunk held tightly with golden hinges. I carry the fading feelings to the edge of all that is holy and paint metallic angels before the bright morning arrives and life begins again.

He Dreamt of Her

He dreamt of her last night as the early morning sun crept into the salmon colored dawn painting the hills. As the coyote voiced its last wail, he sensed her essence in images of a softly flowing rill and in the smooth face of a translucent pond. Paint rushed through his veins as he attempted to create pictures of her fading spirit. A frog croaked from within hidden cracks of russet colored shale in the caverns of his mind and he heard her voice echoing through the mist. He tried to smear a soft pastel wash over the blood-colored reality of his dream world, but a portal opened, revealing only a dark mound of earth. A carved statue of a small marble angel headstone flooded into his memory like tumultuous waves over dark rocks on the seashore, and he wept… again.

He Thinks of Her

He thinks of her, waking up in the gray mist of an anxious morning, her silhouette vulnerable, untouched by the dash of printer's ink upon torn ecru parchment where he penned his poem. Her voice was like the pulses of rain upon the windowsill, fading in intensity as the winds abated into the darkness of the past. He whispers his sad daybreak song as the fog settles into the damp soil… too many months… too many sad mornings. He looks into the mirror, looking into another mirror… searching the vanishing darkness of eternity. She can no longer be touched; she is only an empty reflection in his mind. The barren room rises up as he turns and watches the yellow sun crawl over the hills far in the distance. He would fly away beyond the painted clouds if he could; flee to be with her in the place where she resides… an oaken casket, deep within the earth.

Do Not Be Weary

Whatever is... was; whatever will be... will be.

In the morning's crimson dawn, the eye awakens;
In the evening's scarlet dusk, the eye sleeps.
Meaning has no reality without the eye;
Reality has no meaning without the eye.
The essence of meaning lies within the eye...
Only the eye's sunlight evokes reality.

Justice devoid of mercy is blind;
Mercy devoid of justice is deaf.
Who takes a life is without justice;
Who condemns another is without mercy.

The eye brings the morning dew and
The ornate birds that sing sweet songs;
It brings the laughter of children and
The wisdom of the aged; it is always
Seeing, even when it sleeps... do not
Be weary.

My Valentine Love

Someday when you are older and the days are shorter, you will be nodding by a cozy fire in the Ben Franklin, reading my poems and reminiscing about riding horses and planting herbs in your garden's warm loam. I will be watching you from across the room, you with soft gray hair, brown eyes, and a beautiful smile.

I have always loved you, and now more than ever as you change into the soft glow of aging loveliness. I look into your pleasant face and soft brown eyes that have always sparkled and I see a loving wisdom gleaming from within, and once again know why I loved you so much in the past, love you more now, and will love you even more in the far distant future.

The End of a Day

The tired and worn hours of the day tumble into the sunset as the turbulent waves crest upon the ebony hued rocks on the ocean's shore. The sun dips softly, silently into the magenta horizon as terns and gulls forage frantically to savor the last of the tide's tasty morsels before blackness envelops the cooling sand. The dark seashore—with memories of the day falling over the cliff's edge into the past—slumbers and dreams of a sunny tomorrow when laughing children will once again visit and create new memories.

Change, creation… time: the ever-moving current of the vast ocean always receding and emerging, continually bringing new possibilities to the shoreline and our weary minds. The cooling sea, with its white waves breathing into the night, roars at the pomegranate moon to tell the ocean's angels to come ashore and bless the land. Far out in the vast black sea, the whales bellow to the stars to silence the moan of weary travelers, move the world a bit slower so children can catch up with their dreams and mothers can gather meaning from the hours of the demanding world and their tedious day in order to gain courage for the coming of another morn.

Winter's Scene

From the front porch,
Miles to the east,
Green mountains
Materialize to fill my eyes.
To my left,
Barren, leafless trees
Waiting for spring,
Among their branches
Sparrows longing for
The return of warm days.

An Autumn Evening

In the vanishing twilight of the fall evening, when the sky is the color of coral fading into a dusky pinkish gray, I watch house sparrows squabbling over remaining birdseeds. The tiny painted green house hanging from a limb on a birch tree outside the kitchen window sways in the breeze of the evening hour. A blue jay appears and scatters the nervous sparrows to the barren trees behind the house. A slight breeze ruffles the remaining brown leaves on the trees, sounding like the crinkling of old parchment. The earth, parched from the summer sun and the heat, emerges from the scorching Indian summer winds, begging for moisture. Fall arrives disguised in the form of a sweltering summer day: Everything except for the hot breeze is still. The sparrows eventually return to eat the remaining seeds, and I go inside to the coolness of my house.

Peace

Feelings suffused the ocean with corroded silk lace,
Shattered leaden windows caused feelings of dread
As the sea's emerald current flowed a blood red:
A darkened world headed to Armageddon with haste,
Oily waters of greed flowed with greed's fetid waste:

Horrific hordes of anger buried the bloodied dead,
The blue, naked sky hid gory battles still far ahead,
While the starters of wars became rich… in disgrace.

Rise up, you weary souls without Nero's power:
Allow the inner sun of integrity and morality soar,
Create peace and a scented white rose on a bower:
Allow war-weary men to stop the bloody war;
Allow maidens with smiling souls to plant a flower.

Irises in the Lea

As I was quietly ambling in the woods,
I saw beautiful pink irises under an old
Sycamore tree; they were seemingly
Humming a silent tune. The purple
Flowers were plentiful as leaves on
The old maple tree, which offered them
Healing shade. I relaxed amid their
Beauty while red and yellow flowers
Nearby emitted stunning fragrances
Into the balmy autumn breeze and my
Yearning senses.

Innocent Senses

Ancient sealed doors in the mind
Can only be opened by those with
Innocent senses. Lovely bouquets
Scattered in by whisperings of long
Gone scents of roses and earthy
Odors unbolt pleasant memories
Locked in these sealed doors.

When new aromas emanate
From sweet flowers in the damp
Earth, ancient visions appear to
Waken echoes of the past in our
Soul's eyes. It is only then that
The sealed doors are opened and
We are able to accept life's
Wondrous possibilities waiting
For us in the gentle softness of a
Magenta-tinted morn.

The Poet

His gentle hands write sweet
Poems for those with saddened
Souls: soft words to crumble dark
Epitaphs of grief... poetic prayers in
Shiny graphite. And for those
Not ready for blessings, those
With empty hearts, he plants
Rhythmic flowers with beautiful
Aromas in their gardens of weeds
And showers them with a choired,
Rapturous joy.

The River

As I walked along the dusty path near
the lazy flowing river, I noticed rows
of cattail reeds fading into the vanishing
coral dusk, brown tufted messages
whispering secrets to the dark blue
stream. The holy stalks of unambiguous
character stared at the blueness of
the sky overflowing with tenuous clouds,
forcing me to remember the past.

The lazy flowing river
vanished into the far horizon…
miles and miles of tedious moisture
curling around soft corners of loam,
leading to an obscure cacophony of melodious ripples
and ending in a lake as smooth as glass,
where a small towheaded boy and his father
once sat in an old rowboat, fishing for an ancient trout.

Churches and Shops

A fall breeze whispered across the dusty lane, bouncing withered leaves into the balmy air. The sun slowly moved diagonally in the cloudy sky toward noon as mission bells tolled for the faithful and unfaithful to come to the final mass of the day.

At noon, a priest—in his heavy Irish voice—would attempt to calm the fears of the sinful sitting silently below colorful leaden windows. The saints peered down from the windows with eyes of pious pity on the sinners below.

Down the road from the church, travelers of various hues and voices flocked like lost sheep to Danish bakeries. Heavenly aromas floating in the breeze promising tasty, sugary morsels coaxed them inside.

Doves singing in their odd voices fluttered in the wind like runaway kites above the church bells. They cried for people to come inside and partake in the heavenly cup and divine bread.

Shop owners with smiles and greetings called to the people on the brick sidewalks to partake in the goods in their shops. The happy tourists lured by the shop clerks in Danish costumes entered the shops of diverse sundries to purchase trinkets to take home, and eventually, in a month, forgot they put them in a cluttered drawer along with trinkets from another time.

Poignant parishioners, with atonement in their hearts, sank to their knees on padded pews in the dimmed apse to purchase forgiveness. They believed in the golden transformative miracles offered, but due to human weakness, would forget their promises not to commit the same sins again once they arrived home.

Weep Not, Robin

Weep not, Robin…
For peace comes on summer's wings
As bards write poems to overcome
Your sadness. Wipe away your
Tragic tears from your lonesome being;
Awaken in your heart a sudden gladness.

Weep not, Robin…
For Eirene's warm embrace
Will take you to higher and
Higher splendors of peace,
Expunge the dim world of your
Darkened rhyme under the bountiful
Bouquet of a rose-covered arbor.

Weep not, Robin…
Eleos will break the spell of your
Darkened night and enclose in your
Heart a gleaming halo at dawn. She will
Bring into your being a blissful delight,
And into your soul she will create a
Rebirth and a sweet song.

The White Rose

Oh, gentle white rose quietly enduring the unhurried day, counting the closing minutes of the fading magenta sun as you emit sugary aromas from buds so sweet, worry not; for soon the journey to the horizon's closing stages will be over.

Oh, anxious people whose quest is only for golden metallic things, too many of you pine away with thoughts of tomorrow while failing to enjoy today's heavenly garland of gentle hours, and pining for new things when old things are so beautiful.

We walk from the balmy breeze into the icy gale far too soon. By forgetting the aroma of the white rose, we dig earthen graves while we are yet children. Future things for which we fervently strive can turn to gray ashes while our soul is still in its infancy.

Continually enjoy the fragrance of each white rose along life's way, before the sun dips into the stone gray horizon and you are buried under a cement tomb.

Beach Day

The briny breeze streaming across the heated sand dampens the screeching voices of hungry gulls soaring down from the cliffs to snag tasty morsels on the shore brought in by the never-ending tide. Echoes of happy children's voices and whispers of the elderly bounce off the rocks protruding from the sea as the dark waters moisten the shoreline. The heated sand welcomes the incoming tide as it listens to the giddy screams of children romping in the surf. Memories flood the minds of their mothers and fathers watching the scene with a soft nostalgia.

Separation

The garden, light green and silent, a living essence separating trees from gritty driveway, and something much more… or much less; a living, verdant boundary between austere memories and jovial dreams, between the laughter of youth and the moans of the aging. I hear voices troubled by storms and ills and those with deep worries, and scatter the discordant remains among the flowers to break their monotony in the dark soil. I water the flowers with voices infused with laughter and gaiety to bring out the beauty of colors and scents of perfumed fragrance. I build brick paths so others may stroll among the loveliness of the garden that separates laughter from weeping.

Sleep

Sleep eludes me; hides within the discordant
caverns of my soul where only crimson
whispers live, where enigmatic metaphors
mingle with blurred visions in the dark hours
of the night… I walk on miseries of splintered
glass. A gloomy song's musical chords crackle
like crystal leaves falling upon a cobblestone
path.

A night bird suddenly sings, a frog croaks in
the shadows, and my waking nightmares sink
into obscurity. The soft murmurings of the night
cause my fears to fall into the moon's
luminescence as golden angels in a melodious
harmony turn darkness into light, then an
aria of translucent serenity overcomes my
fears and I finally sleep.

Christmas

Colorful elves hiding behind Christmas packages in the rear of
    the divan,
Not making a sound in the hesitant night as they craft a plum-
    laden plan,
An owl outside in the dim reflection of the moon labors with the
Gray dove to create a special Noel night colorfully painted with
    songs of love.

Dappled warty frogs croaking happily in the horses' troughs
As tiny gray mice dance in the larder wearing red calico cloths.
Children in their warm beds dreaming visions of that special gift
As green tendrils of ivy laced with red ribbons crawl up the lift.

The grandfather with an ancient black and red Indian flute
Plays a lopsided song, dressed in a velvet Santa Claus suit.
Happy visions of long-past seasons stream 'cross his wrinkled
    brow;
Images of a pine tree, and sprigs with aromatic scents that endow.

Then in the flicker of an eye, Christmas morning is here to entice,
And excited children bound down the stairs, scurrying the mice.
The Christmas tree glitters with bows and gold, while presents
    galore
Fill the living room, the hallway, and the old hutch's big drawer.

After the presents are unwrapped and the children are at play,
The parents and grandparents start talking their singular way,
The turkey goes into the oven to bake and the table is set for the
    feast,
And excited anticipation of the exceptional holy night is
    increased.

The time finally arrives and all sit down for a holy blessing,
Then share the turkey, potatoes, cranberry sauce, and dressing.
After a toast with an aged wine, the feast begins with content
      sighs,
And the partakers find their stomachs are smaller than their eyes.

The Album

Upon his death,
The day in its
Pomegranate hew
Faded into
The droning voice
Of lost reminiscences.

Bleak, transparent…
Diminishing
Into rusted hours,
The church
Void of sound,
Like the flailing
Of butterfly wings.

Lonely people
Congregating
With damp tissues and
Silence…
The wooden casket stark…
Unflinching.

And… those
Who knew him?
Noticed a peculiar absence,
A life gone…
But in time,
Only a vanishing memory.

Eventually
Only a faded picture
Would remain

In a dusty
Picture album
Of other dead relatives...

But... where is immortality?

I Am

I am a peculiarity which feels earthen
tones in the midst of contemporary
metallic hues, a denunciation in the
kingdom of void, a feeling soul among
plastic beings with green hearts, a tear
flowing sadly alongside the agony of
the living and dying. An eye that weeps
at the sight of starving children, fallen
women, discarded people in foreign
lands, and bodies of soldiers in alien
nations.

I am that oddity that wears tee
shirts with Franz Kafka on the front and
Jane Austen on the back. I am a dream
filled with the clashing of empty
questions replied with nonsensical
existential answers, a Kierkegaardian
riddle encompassing the darkness of the
earth roaming in the ashes of a volcano
that will erupt weeping in the soiled
alleys of the homeless. I am a non-
luminous projection of unreality that
attempts to contradict the paradoxical
awareness of the existence of disbelief.

I am an aging soul searching the
panoramas of the past for the serenity of
future vistas, a dark specter searching
for the light in the laughter of a small
child; I am a naivety probing for the
aroma of a single white rose that no

longer exists on an ancient arbor, and
an essence in search of spiritual
answers in trash dumps filled with the
scent of philosophers and the fibers of
the brown robes of the religious. I am a
hollow mind seeking the glow of reality,
a body wearing into rust, a wisp of wind
floating carelessly in the hurricane of
chaos.... A lonely soul filled with incredible
questions involving the reasons for my
existence.

I am a leaf blowing on the
ripples of frozen streams; a bag of
bones held together by frozen hope, and
an implausible image of that which is
curiously enigmatic and inexplicable.

I am much like you.

The Weight of Silence

The weight of silence is pure emptiness, the song it sings is heard only in the vast void of that which is incomprehensible; its moral imperatives concern the true essence of that which extends beyond explanation. When it arrives on the back of thunderous white-crested waves, nothing is heard but the roar of breaking waves... but there, deep inside the turmoil, waiting for ears that can't hear it, is silence. The absence of silence is never found in earthly objects, or in the streets of the world; it is only found in the caverns of those things which are ephemeral. Listen closely to silence and you will unlock the answers to the enigmas of life.

Nostalgia

It's past midnight in a shadowy bar in a small town called Someplace; a young man in Levis and a 24-hour beard is playing a sorrowful rusted harmonica while an older man in a black fedora is singing a sad 60's folk song in a whiskey-painted voice.

Something inside a young man's soul stirs… something beyond the jazz music playing harmoniously in the darkness, beyond the whispering clarinet and crimson silhouettes sitting at oaken tables, hanging on to a last chance. It is something larger than magic, more obscure; it goes beyond the rhythmic beat, the sad saxophone now singing in the corner of the tavern, and the low, heartbreaking voice of the chanteuse in the mini scarlet dress swaying next to the microphone; it is beyond the gravel voice of the man playing the electric guitar in a rusty G major to the rear.

Memories flood the man's mind like ocean waves bursting onto jagged rocks; tears tumble down his cheeks as visions of the past curve around his lonely mind, leaving a nostalgic feeling in his bones that he cannot deny. He looks down the bar and sees her… long red hair, a beautiful poignant face reflecting crimson regrets. Her glance and coy smile paint crimson feelings into his soul. He starts to move, but something inside stops him as he remembers another time, another place, another young woman... a long, long time ago.

Dreams on a Wintry Night

Pleasurable images have washed this way,
Thoughts are hushed and serenely still,
They live peacefully in dreams at night.

In colored glass the shade of whey,
Thoughts echo calmly from my quill;
Pleasurable images have washed this way.

In the middle of a snowy winter day
They rise from behind a whitened hill;
They live peacefully in dreams at night.

Contented feelings are those that stay
Around the window's whitewashed sill:
Pleasurable images have washed this way.

In the brightness of the sunny way
Where destiny fulfills everyone's will,
They live peacefully in dreams at night.

Darkness will no longer dismay,
In tranquil minds away from the chill,
Pleasurable images have washed this way;
They live peacefully in dreams at night.

Shades of Red

Ruby-tinted words skulk along the sides of Garnet metaphors in places where lyrics die of shame and nouns bounce off the Crimson edges of my mind. Dark well-read tomes line the heaviness of my sinking bookcases. Strident songs of gaudy birds parting from Carnelian beaks stream into my ears, reminding me of the cackling of titled dames flaunting Raspberry-colored diamonds and Carmine decorated inanities, slurping champagne cocktails at a gala for poor underprivileged orphans.

A sea of Vermillion currents covers my aspirations in a frozen moment of angelic smoke; with hidden fears in hand, I cross the Cerise-painted river that follows me whenever the Paprika sun unfolds into the quickly forming morn. In my head, shapeless talons of incomprehension dig deeply into my Pomegranate memories that are layered with regrets. I fear the arrival of the Maroon mist hovering… hovering… hovering in the vanishing Red glow of my unfinished story. My bones feel the chill of the Cardinal-hued past; my fading mind senses the closing of the door, the shutting of the window, the opening of a Scarlet abyss, a hole so deep a city of absurdities could hide in it forever. I am weary of the Coral hours that bind me to the past, the Burgundy days that fall too quickly from the hurried pace of life. Where is peace for those of evaporating years, trying to delay the dank earthen hole and cement tomb? Everything is vanishing too fast as I sit with only my Magenta-tainted past to keep me company.

There is Beauty in the World

Walking on a dusty deer path with my dark anger and troublesome fears close beside me, I suddenly see autumn leaves falling and crackling, sounding like crystal feet on old yellow parchment; the sound and colors enter my ears and capture my eyes. I breathe in the brisk fresh air and search for answers in the colorful foliage; find whisperings of gentle emotions floating with the leaves in the breeze. A tiny, softly flowing rill covered with yellow leaves and grassy moss murmurs rippling rhymes that reach into my being.... I watch and listen as I cross a small oaken bridge over the rill... my anger and fears are lagging far behind me now.

My senses start to awaken to all that is beautiful; I follow ancient wooden steps that take me to the top of a verdant knoll. It is there that I discover serenity and a sudden calmness overwhelms my soul. I hear a frog stirring in the rill below; it croaks a soft guttural verse into my mind, soothing away my remaining fears. I find peace on top of the verdant knoll of beautiful sweet-smelling wild roses and purple lilacs resting under a sycamore tree reaching for heaven. I sit silently among the wild flowers and my worldly troubles vanish; my heart no longer aches. Why does it take man so much time to recognize that which is so simple to realize... that there is so much beauty and tranquility in the world?

Promise on a Summer Day

To be with you on this summer day and
Listen to verdant leaves that whisper
Songs of love, downy birds that warble
Poems of affection, to observe butter
Yellow butterflies flitting under giant
White-barked sycamore trees where
Only a soft breeze can be felt. When the
Sunlight caresses your face and the
Gentle breeze combs your auburn hair,
I know I can only be in love with you
And no one else. I yearn to hold you
Closer as each new day welcomes us
With its golden glow. I promise to never
Depart, never leave your side. When the
Din of humanity can no longer be heard,
Only the beat of your heart, I will
Embrace you in my arms and kiss your lips;
Then I will take you in my arms as the ocean
Holds the current in its briny grip, as the sky
Holds misty clouds in its bluish hands, as the
Fertile mountains hold streams in an earthly grasp,
I will embrace you eternally in my heart, and
My love will last forever.

Summer

Summer visions come this way,
The ocean's tide calm and still:
The freezing winter is now at bay.

Barren trees no longer dismay,
My heart will stay calm until
Summer visions come this way.

Icy nights, cold days decay,
Mountains without winter's chill;
The freezing winter is now at bay.

Unfriendly winds do not sway,
Obscuring warmth by iceman's will;
Summer visions come this way.

Unfriendly gusts not due today,
Blowing warm thoughts from the hill;
The freezing winter is now at bay.

Soon warm winds will come to stay,
The sun will reflect on the rill,
Summer visions come this way, and
The freezing winter is now at bay.

Escape to the Woods

An escape to the woods is the only salvation in a world filled with travail and war. I wander on dusty paths near a rugged flowing brook, smiling at every flower I see, smelling the sweet aroma of their breath. In every song by feathered beast, I sense no cry of fear; unlike man, whose sighs are hapless moans of daily woes. I watch in silence as a timid doe eats the sweet grass far to my left. As I watch, I worry about those of humankind who hunger for lack of food in the hot sands of a refugee camp.

I sit on the pebbly sand by a tranquil pond and listen to the guttural sighs of dappled frogs sitting among the reeds, and worry about soldiers who have no place to lay their weary heads. As the balmy breeze fills flowered fields with sweet aromas and odors of wild things large and small, my mind swallows up visions of pleasurable things, but my soul, worn with man's troubles, still wanders on the dusty trails of sadness.

He Was

He was once
a thinker of
things of the mind,
a taster of metallic
ideas,
a believer of things
unknown,
a student of
the dark and light
in the wee hours
of the night,
a person that
lived in the
spirit of the
past, a dreamer,
a feeling person
amidst the
unfeeling, lost
in the misplaced essence
of justice and
mercy. He has
now vanished into
the shadows of
earthen memories.

Mass

The bronze bells in the old tower pealed for mass; the faithful and unfaithful alike streamed into the apse like pebbles being carried downstream by a slow-moving current.

Some walked in silence, others with muffled words hanging onto the ears of their fellow parishioners. The wind outside chilly… inside a welcoming warmth.

Rows of shiny oaken pews separated by the red carpet sea beckon parishioners and travelers.

The light dim, minds hushed. The hour approaches then stops for breath as the cross, held high, starts down the aisle.

All stand in reverence as the priest in his bright gold Alb walks behind the cross. The old man and woman in the second row bow as Jesus looks down on them from the cross.

The woman, pure as the linen on the altar, stands beside her husband holding his hand, both aware of that which was ending and that which faced them in the future.

Their hearts held the keys to the past, their souls to the future. Like thin crystal statues trapped under the trapdoors of the word, they knelt upon the padded kneelers and prayed for another day.

Their fears disappeared down the caverns of their imaginations as they listened to the priest's incantations, their bodies purified with the body and blood.

In the Garden at Dawn

In the early morning as I walk meandering paths in my garden under the ancient sky, my imagination grows with colorful images while roses emit their perfumed fragrance into the atmosphere. Orange and yellow zinnias paint the area with Monet surrealism about absent friends and lasting love. A gentle feeling surrounds me like a multihued feather comforter as rhymes flow from the beds of pink irises filled with affection, Canterbury bells with a blue constancy, Larkspur's open heart, and Queen Anne's Lace's fantasies. I wander on the paths of crushed redwood chips, soft upon my feet, and eavesdrop on the tiny new vegetable plants starting to emerge in my old wooden planters. The song in my aging mind sings along with the singsong chattering of meadowlarks, the odd cooing of ring-tailed doves, and the soft chirping of warblers and titmice. The sun crawls languidly over the hills to the east and I feel the warmth slowly falling upon the garden. It is a good start to another day; an important day... I am alive.

Nature's Tranquility

The languid sun creeps gradually over the mountains to the east, painting the verdant valley below with a soft orange hue; a new day rouses from the darkness of the night. The mountain brook lazily flowing down its rocky bed reflects the sun off of leaves of orange and yellow fallen from sycamore trees. Downy birds begin to sing their warbled songs as they fly to and fro from tree to tree, searching for bugs for breakfast. A doe and her fawn nibble gently at green grass in the meadow, watching with ears fluttering for intruders. The old man pauses to take in the peaceful scene and sighs. His wooden cane by his side trembles slightly as he leans on it for support. So many years, so many years... and the beautiful landscape of nature never varies; it continues on season after season, year after year, always offering visions of pleasure. So much turmoil in the battered world, so many troubles, so many hurting, yet in this natural world, beauty and tranquility reign.

A Wooded Place

His thoughts reflected in broken visions, his mind mulls over the world in cryptic dullness. He lives in a fading awareness where images are shattered into jigsaw bits of the past and present, his mind heavy with a leaden haze, his soul lost in images of the past. The old man stumbles painfully down the sandy lane, realizing this trek may be his last. He sighs in sadness. So much to do, so little time left. Days fly by like minutes, years like months, images... lost visions shattered into pieces of crystal upon the cobblestones of his life. He looks to his left and sees a doe nibbling on fresh new grass; to his right, a squirrel sits up with an acorn in its mouth. In front of him lands a blue jay pecking at bugs in the grass, nonchalant of his existence. He pauses from the darkness within and his mind emerges into the light to concentrate on the beauty of the meadow displayed in front of him. He smells the aroma of wild flowers and the damp earth. He looks to heaven and prays for a few more years to enjoy the peacefulness and beauty of this wooded place. He smiles as the sun peeks out from behind the clouds and places beams of warmth on his head.

Ashen Bones

Often, beneath the rolling waves in the blue sea, the ashen bones of drowned men cover sea creatures also long dead. The pulse of their memories beat upon the sandy shore, hidden and obscure without the pious peal of holy bells. Shattered chapters unread, in bloody ink, heralding the lives of those with deadly wounds, their frozen eyes watching visions of malice striking golden altars with flames. Upon the shore, urchins dig into the sand, scattering tiny bits of food and bone while the roar of the surf, like Thor's thunder, beats like a mighty hammer upon the incoming tide. The great glint of eternity keeping a log of such things for future minds to ponder, winks at the lustrous stars as the human remains scatter under the sea to swollen entrances covering the past of bent promises, to no avail. With eyes toward heaven and over pillaged gilded pillars of stone, they presumed hopes would drift like a communion of faith into the heavenly altar of Eden, where holy sacraments would be found upon a banished tree. But, alas, the silent encroachment of death, the tribunal sovereign of the darkness, smiled and slew without remorse, leaving only ashen bones for someone to ponder someday in the far future while sitting on the shore of some lonely beach.

How & Where

How

Do you read a poem
That was never written, or
Hear a song that was
Never sung, or revisit a place
You have never been?

How

Do you write a poem
That has no lyrics, or visit
A friend you never had, or
Find colorful memories that
Never existed except in gray?

How

Do you find dreams
Lost in the gray miasma
Of past years, or a love that
Never existed except in
The caverns of your
Fantasizing mind?

Where

Do you go when
You are lost in yesterday and
Have no place to go today, or
Find answers to questions
You dared never ask?

Where

Can you find solace
In a chaotic and damaged
World, when the stones
Under your feet have turned
To crimson-colored thorns?

Where

Can you hide when it is all over, and
There is nothing left except
People crying and your
Corpse is rotting in a crumbling
Cement tomb?

Cry Not, My Love

Cry not, my love;
Warmth arrives on summer's wings.
It will bring rhymes to overcome
Your sorrow, wash away sad
Tears from your abandoned being,
Rouse in your heart a rapid joy.

Cry not, my love;
Amid a rose-covered arbor
In my loving embrace, your
Happiness will ascend in a
Radiance of hopeful fervor,
Obliterating the day of its gloomy
Rhyme, producing profuse aromas.

Cry not, my love;
I will fracture the curse of the unlit night,
Encircle your soul with a luminous halo,
And bring into your heart a blissful
Gladness; and into your soul, I will build
A renaissance and a sweet song.

Stooping in the Fields

All day long, Maria stoops to the dull cadence of
A song of hopelessness flitting through her mind.

The young girl with long braided black hair and
Olive cheeks longs for things common to others:

An education, a separate bedroom in a warm
House, days without backbreaking labor

Picking vegetables for those with tables filled
With delicious food and laughter.

I pity her toiling in the vast, unforgiving hot fields
Of dark loam hour after hour, day after day,

Month after month, always wondering if there is
A balcony in a white two-story stucco house in a

City somewhere, where she could look down on
A beautiful garden of flowers and dreams, and

Then retreat into a warm house with a table filled
With delicious food and laughter.

The Herb Garden

She dwelt upon the silence in her garden of herbs as she pushed the trowel deeply into the soft loam. In her hand a clay pot holding tightly to a sprig of mint, a smile crossed her lips as she shook out the plant and placed it in the welcoming cavity. Her bare roses to the west already sprouting dark scarlet leaves, a fresh bouquet of harmonious aromas will drift from them in a month, her pink irises already in the budding stage ready to open to the breath of spring. She pauses and takes in the serenity of her garden and her trowel digs deep into the soil to create a hole for another herb.

Aging

Dried feathers hanging loosely on a metaphor,
Cacophonous notes glued together with iambic age,
Partners in the rhyming crime of the toxic
Thing called the golden years. I yearn for the
Sweet aroma of yellow roses sitting inside
A vase filled with youthful longings in
The light of a pomegranate sky. I cling to the
Past of black and white movies, drive-ins, and
29 cent hamburgers. Oh, to be young again and
Not have wrinkles, gray hair, shuffling feet,
And vanishing memories.

I Am Worn

I am worn from constant
striving, and the raucous
din of cities filled with
neon lights and crimson
sin, I am tired of grubby
streets and greedy
men, drained from
Angry people painted
with patience thin.

I am ready for verdant
meadows and a wooded
glen, for colorful birds
singing tender songs to
lonely old men; I am
anxious to discover air
pure and thin, and
discover sandy paths
with animals lacking an
anger within.

Sweet Aromas

The flowers upon the windowsill waft their beautiful aroma throughout the room, a purer scent man cannot or manufacture for his tomb. Pine trees carry a dove's soft voice so clear, so traveler and homebound alike will listen with a heartfelt ear.

An Observation

When I was very young, I watched the moon's essence splash down in a moonbeam from the vastness of space. Its magic dust glittered into my open mind. As I grew older, I was told the moon was a mere orb of dead earth that takes up space.

In my later youth, I still often wondered about the magic of the moon's halo, before I was tainted by living and now by dying. It was once a vision of wonder, an invitation to ponder love and life. The moon seemed then like a sphere filled with hopefulness wearing a happy face. As I grew older, I found it was just a cold hunk of metal, an earth with pockets of craters; all the magic vanished with age. The mystery disappeared, too, weighed down with calculus and physics and too many years of learning, all of which caused the fantasy to disappear.

I looked yesterday out the window at the moon's halo and saw an angel smiling at me through a diaphanous cloud floating above the earth. I once again felt the shiver of mystery and the old fantasy began to materialize in my mind. I shifted my weight in my bed where I was confined and moved my body so the magic dust of the moonbeams would envelop me. As I gazed at the moon, the essence of the moonbeams infused into my mind and I smiled.

If only we could continue to feel the creative pull of the magic moon in the middle of our lives—when we are busy accumulating unnecessary things—instead of just in the beginning and ending of life... we would then never lose our childish ability to feel and create wonders in our minds.

Regrets

Last night I dreamt that I had died. When the morning arrived, I found myself in an oaken casket sitting under the gray soil of a sad spring day's mist. I thought about all the things I was supposed to do for you today: mow the lawn, fix the broken gutter, clean the garage, wash the car, fix the leaking hose, take out the garbage which had started to smell under the kitchen sink, buy some Elmer's glue to fix your favorite tea cup I dropped last Monday, and say I am sorry for yelling at you last night, especially for yelling at you last night, especially for yelling at you last night… My regrets stream across my excuses... do you hear them?

The Poet's Night

When the sun quickly fades
And the glow in the land is dead,
The night brings in dark shades;
The garden's color is shed.

When the golden flute is still,
Its sweet voice soon forgot,
The darkness brings a chill;
Love songs come to naught.

Colors and songs do not live long
In the emptiness of sun and flute,
In the starless night, hope is gone,
The bard's voice is always mute.

When there is only the ebony dark,
No beautiful color or song can be felt;
The color of wishes goes suddenly
Stark, the poems in our soul quickly melt.

The poet hidden from color and light
Writes lyrics of a darkened theme,
Weeps for white linen paper to write
New thoughts unblackened by a bleak
Dream. He frantically pens into the late night
Hours, attempting to overcome things
That scream; he steals happiness from
A scented bower, tries to scatter chaos
From its extremes.

He continues to create throughout the
Night, then as the sun peeks over

From Mother East, his heart gladdens in
The new sun so bright, his mind relaxes;
He is rid of the beast.

He is no longer beholding to the gloom,
The dark thing that held captive his
Heart; his spirit is now free to awaken
And bloom, giving his poet's life a sunny new start.

What objects were the wishes of his
Nightly strain; what rhythms did he pen
In his darkest pain? He searches before
And then after, and in his soul finds a
Lilting laughter in the garden knoll as
The flute plays a melody and the new
Day tolls.

The Train

In the cold north wind,
    Memories slowly flow
From the iron horse
    As it slowly disappears into the
Dark, unforgiving space
    Of unbending time.

The Inexplicable

Philosophers continually attempt, without success, to explain that which is inexplicable, to decipher the DNA of God's mind as it constantly morphs from omniscience into obscurity, from the covertly hidden into that which is overtly plain and back again. The hand of figurative darkness extinguishes the flame of significance when man uses complex semantics of symbols to solve the paradoxes that enter into his soul… that thing which has no meaning but contains all meaning.

From where do we go to find sanity in such an inscrutable world, from where do we find mercy in an unjust world; from where do we find love in the bowls of evil? Only when we answer those enigmatic questions will we have peace.

The Soldier and His Girl

As the minutes of their last night were quickly fading and silver moonbeams caressed her face, his trembling hand softly caressed her auburn hair.

Holding her tightly, he listened to her fears and, grasping her trembling hand, kissed the lines etched upon her worried brow. Sitting quietly, he tried to salvage the precious time left without the sounds of bullets and foreign words. He held her as the sea holds the tide in its salty hands. As he embraced her, he silently prayed for one more precious minute before he had to get on that lonely train and head back to the bloody war.

A Special Morn

It was a special orange-tinted morn…
Cheerful, still, as peaceful as a lea's
Hushed dell, as the sun's beams cast
A sacred spell, it thawed my soul from
The frigid chill. As gaudy birds sang
Near a placid rill, their voices in my
Mind quietly dwelled; my soul rejoiced,
My worries were quelled, in my ears
Their songs delicately trilled.

My lover's hand I caringly grasped;
Holding my breath, I kissed her compliant
Lips; with my pulse madly beating, I
Held her near, gave her a teak box
With a golden hasp, earnestly promising
Her manors and majestic ships, swearing
Her life would be happy and never austere.

A New Morn

Remnants of the dark night gone away
Now colored orange with the creation of morn;
Memories of shadowy dreams no longer shrill.

The gloomy vestiges of darkness sway,
Warm zephyrs in my soul are born;
Remnants of the dark night have gone away.

Happy thoughts being born today,
Darkness being blown and torn;
Memories of shadowy dreams no longer shrill.

The warmth of a yellow rising sun will stay,
Past memories no longer forlorn;
Remnants of the dark night have gone away.

I welcome the heat of the sun's loyal ray,
Into my open heart it flows untorn;
Memories of shadow dreams no longer shrill.

Only ashen bits of darkness still dismay
In this happy place amid rows of golden corn;
The remnants of the dark night have gone away,
Memories of shadow dreams no longer shrill.

The Blue Jay

The mighty blue jay, with its feathered attitude of importance, coasts into the feeding birdhouse like an azure robbed phantom, scattering the shy house sparrows to the trees. It looks around and shows its imperial stance at all who attempt to intrude upon its catered delicacies. Like ermine-covered women at a gala strutting colored diamonds and imperial postures, it creates an aura of entitled regal importance.

A Sonnet to the Past

When my memories begin to hastily fade
In the dull grayness of the skies hoary gray,
I fear that sleepless days would crawl away
Into the absurdity of thoughts sorely mislaid,
Covering sweet promises I once had made and
Unwinding the special times, now gone astray.
As the moon spins its hopeful glow my way,
I revel in the pure beauty of a muse's parade;
I see the glint of a pleasing rhyme be born.
Oh, that my mind could go back to that year
To hear the sweet melody of that French horn,
Experience the golden laughter and good cheer,
The melodious sounds of mirth still unborn,
And listen closely to golden songs so dear.

A Sonnet for Sad Times

Oh, to forget the moaning sounds of that day
Which trumpeted the hours of a lonely morn,
Dampened the lives of those so wretchedly torn.
Allow sadness to fade into memories far away,
Consent to peaceful hours to cover the deathly gray;
Create a heavenly sense of hope to be reborn,
Permitting sad, grieving minds to endure the thorn
And thrust Death's splintering voice far astray.
Then on some new bright and cheerful night,
Allow those with splintered hearts to heal,
Permit their broken heart's reddened scar
To fail to remember that which is contrite,
Fling thoughts of the grievous loss upon a star
And consent to let joyful hours to congeal.

Finally... Sleep

In my wakened dream-mind a collection of memories appears, among them experiences only vaguely imagined, visions collectively realistic—by themselves absurd—their plum juicy hands fondle my ashen bones amid gnarled and rusted metaphors. Below the darkness, a mystic's voice emerges from behind the sun's halo of fire; speaking in a forgotten language, she calls my name. From inside a corroded eddy, I see my image molded from broken promises, condensing into formless utterances of fantasies. My dreaming senses like gateways surrounded by a panorama of voices, skulls, and feathers as ocean waves and waterfalls noisily beckon to me. I imagine possibilities without form inhaled by my pores through golden spider webs. The heavens open and the moisture emitted from translucent clouds, like rushing waves, talks to that which is within the possibilities of my being. A silent, transparent lake shimmering like a gathering of stars, an ocean of luminosity, hidden between reality and my fantasies, causes a revelation to appear. I receive the evening's pulsating grace of luminescent purity, and the world's woes enter into indistinctness, allowing me to sleep.

The Fox and the Turtle

An old turtle and a young kit fox met
On a dusty path in the desert.

The fox looked at the turtle and
Asked, "What is in the sack on
Your back, old turtle?"

The turtle answered sadly, "Old memories."

"What do you have in the sack on
Your back, young fox?"

The young fox answered happily, "Dreams."

"Are the memories heavy, old turtle?"

"Oh, yes, very heavy. Are your dreams heavy?"

"Oh, no... they are as light as the clouds in the sky."

The old turtle sighed heavily, looked up at the clouds,
And tried unsuccessfully to remember the times when
He was young and his old memories were still dreams.

A 2014 California Winter

The brown stagnant pond, without a wrinkle, an irregularity present after drought-laden winters; winter rains forgot to give its needed moisture to our parched land, causing the meadows to go fallow and burn.

This was a peaceful spot amid verdant trees that surrounded the once flowing stream bounding with unbridled passion to the lake far below. It is now an area filled with uncommon silence, burned out oaks, hot winds, and thirsting animals. It was once a comforting and serene place where thoughts could lie idle among the countless metamorphic rocks sitting stoically on the gently flowing brook's edges. I touched the heat of the unusual summer day, as past verdant times moved slowly through my memories and my eyes filled with moisture.

I Do Not Understand

I watch a Christian minister burning the Koran
And blaspheming a God
Who is also his,
And I do not understand.

I look into the eyes of a terrorist
Who smiles as he blows apart bodies of innocent mothers
And children in Allah's name,
And I do not understand.

I look into the eyes of an imam,
Who screams to his followers
To kill all who do not believe as he,
And I do not understand.

I look into the eyes of a predator,
Who snuffs out the life of a small child
After abasing her,
And I do not understand.

I look into the eyes of a gang member
As he slashes his knife across the belly
Of a fourteen-year old boy,
And I do not understand.

I look into the eyes of a CEO
As he steals the pensions of his workers
And destroys their futures,
And I do not understand.

I look into the eyes of a politician,
Who has no compassion for those

Who are in need,
And I do not understand.

I look into the hearts of the wealthy
That are without pity for those whose
Labor makes them rich,
And I do not understand.

I look into the soul of a priest,
Who abuses lovely children
In his holy church,
And I do not understand.

I look into the angry minds of those
Who hate others who do not
Think as they do,
And I do not understand.

I look into the mind of the executive,
Who sees beauty only in wealth and not
In poetry, music, or art,
And I do not understand.

I look into the eyes of those who
Make millions by exploiting
The sexuality of others,
And I do not understand.

I look into the eyes of those
Who have no compassion for others,
Who live with lost and hopeless souls,
And I do not understand.

I look into the image in the mirror
That feels helpless to make
A difference in the world,
And I weep because I do not understand.

The Cougar

It was late one dim moonlit night on a hot, muggy summer day when my dog, Nabby, started barking wildly. I took a flashlight, went outside, and gazed around the yard. I started up the dirt road by our house, flashed the light into a huge oak tree, and saw a figure lounging on a limb. At first, I thought it was a raccoon, but as I moved the light along the limb high in the tree, I saw a gorgeous set of dark eyes attached to a large head and tan body looking back at me. I wondered what the female cougar was thinking as her eyes met mine. I stood there as we eyed each other, and after telling her how beautiful she was, slowly turned around and went back toward the house to call animal control. When they finally arrived, the cougar had vanished. I was glad because she was so beautiful and they might have killed her. Maybe someday we will encounter each other again… perhaps in a dream.

The Miniscule Speck in the Heavens

From Saturn, there appears in the dark sky billions of miles away a tiny, luminous dot. It is Earth, an inconspicuous and insignificant isle in the midst of vastness, a tiny crumb of soil and water floating in the darkness of never-ending space. The implication of being such a trivial speck in the vast universe fails to make an impact upon too many minds. Far too often, humans feel their singular greatness and importance is vast and everlasting. How can one not understand that human hands in search of meaningless wealth are destroying the little bit of soil on which we all dwell? What is the importance of the accumulation of *things* if they create toxic air, polluted streams, and contaminated oceans? What is the value of continually amassing worthless objects and trinkets of gold, which are ephemeral? What does man really *need* to live his finite life pleasantly and comfortably? When will humans awaken and grasp the nature of what they are doing to the earth just to amass meaningless gaudy ornaments and baubles of glass? What will our future families have left when this tiny speck of dirt is shattered?

That Time of the Year

Winter is upon us as all can see,
Dark clouds cover hills like a hooded thief.
Turbulent waves grow high in the sea,
Swift winds blow away a rusted leaf.

The sun is low, the mountains green,
Clear water fills the ponds lying low,
Ornaments cover the pine tree lean,
On the pasture falls a soft white snow.

Christmas is coming, 'tis almost here,
Outside greenery and lights hung on the gate,
Children are anxious and of good cheer,
The house is cozy, a fire on the grate.

Madness

There is madness between
Truth and
Duplicity;
A disconnect that I yearn to
Reconnect.
I crave to be that which I can
Not be,
To know
What is
Unknowable.

I decry the darkness of
Unreality and seek
The deep ocean's mysteries,
Which baffle the
Philosopher's and
Scientist's quest for
Certainty.
I dream of a certainty
Which my being
Screams to understand
Without dilution…
I have a hunger which seeks what
Is undiluted and pure.

As I immerse my feelings into
The stillness of the hollows of
My probing soul,
My broken memories spew
Into the ambiguity of inexplicable
Truths.
With my human abstractions,

I listen to the false sirens
Howling in
My seething mind.
Come to me, oh dear certainty,
So I can listen
To your warmth and smell
Truthfulness;
Come to me in the calmness
Of the night, so
I can hear the sound of
Vanishing voices and
Sense the honesty of the
Essence of reality....

Answers

It is said that answers are
Found at every river's end,
Carried by memories from
Deep within;
From every man and
Woman's dream
Comes certainty
Within life's stream.

All events in a single way
Reflect upon the approaches
We use each and every day,
Every hour, every minute
Of all our years,
Bear the bloody scars of
Our darkest fears.

When out of the range of
Sophocles' ear, or
Herodotus' judgmental breath
That we cannot hear,
We search for our countenance
In the aroma of a crimson rose,
And attempt to forget our
Daily woes.

Ancient Earthen Paths

As I leisurely stroll earthen paths,
I hear, in my wistful mind, rocks
Of basalt quoting stony poems
As they sit stoically in the brisk
Fall breeze, watching the endless
Hours arriving and departing
In the whispering wind. Black,
Jagged boulders in their earthen beds
Sit noiselessly, staring blindly at the sky.
Stones and pebbles of agate form rock
Statues by my hand, idols spun of once
Searing earth. Ecru-colored slate, cracked like
Bits of dough, rise from a blue rill's
Moisture then silently plunges back into the
Water, seeking a deep blue eternity.
Frogs croak throaty songs of discord
As they gawk jealously with bulbous eyes
At gaudy fish catching juicy bugs,
Flying carelessly near the river's skin.
Together, blue jays, sparrow hawks, and
Crows singing a medley of cacophonous
Notes suddenly combine in an aria of
Melodious delusion. Grayish white fluffs
Of moisture form huge sculptures of
Mighty ships, stately mansions, and pirates
In the far distance. I then sense nature
Placing her gusty hand on my shoulders,
Telling me warmer times are coming this way.

A Wintry Sea and Lost Memories

Tiny sea creatures in the emerald tide pool
Moved quickly under cold winds of the wintry day,
Their silence ebbing into brackish impossibilities,
Their bulging eyes staring at the fading sun dipping
Slowly into the pink undulating west horizon.
I gathered my thoughts hiding in the miasma
Of the waning day encased in long shadows and
Walked on the damp sand, searching for long
Lost memories.

The current brought in longings forming a frothy,
Yearning brine as it seeped into the sand;
The never-ending tide traveled back and forth
In a salty, rhythmic beat. I listened to seagulls
And terns arguing like petulant children over
Bits of seaweed containing juicy morsels.
The cool day faded into ghosts of more
Balmy times, my nostalgic mind meandered
Into the past… those times when I was young
And felt sorry for myself.

I saw a homeless woman dressed in rags
Scavenging for aluminum cans next to
The shale outcroppings above the shore;
She was shivering in the brisk wind, and
Like the sea birds, was mumbling to
Herself. I wondered to myself if her days
Were ever filled with hopefulness, a warm bed,
Or a full stomach, and suddenly realizing how
Fortunate I was, I shook my head in shame.

The Stranger

A gray, sated shadow of a stranger cast a spell upon the lawn. Cosmic time spread across the grass, each blade drinking in the moisture of the dew; the seconds shifted like a broken dial. From the top of the hill in the distance, shattered beams of light tinted with the scarlet dreams of the fading sun shone on her face. Her voice, like the pealing of a small bronze church bell, asked if I could spare some change. I pulled out a five-dollar bill and handed it to her. I wondered if it would be for a bottle of nightmare-colored alcohol or a hazy blue cigarette, like most of the twenty-somethings of this age and ilk. I then noticed as she smiled and motioned to the buggy on the road. "Thank you, it is for her, she has not had a bottle since this morning." I nodded, feeling shame, and handed her a twenty. The passage, 'Do not judge,' entered my mind and I understood its meaning.

Spring III

Spring has arrived; it's no longer cold,
The bright sun melted winter's icy robe.
Rills flow softly in chasms down the hill,
Dappled green frogs are croaking shrill;
The bright sun creates colors to behold.

I longed eagerly for springtime to unfold,
For I love the aroma of flowers that unfold
And the day's warmth, which removes the chill.
Spring has arrived; it's no longer cold.

After spring, summer is foretold,
In verdant meadows no longer gold.
Velvety birds will sing at their will;
I will visit flowers near a flowing rill,
Watch the birds and animals being bold.
Spring has arrived; it's no longer cold.

Another Summer Gone

The birch tree with brown, dry leaves cites weathered sonnets to the passing breeze, the waning brook quotes damp Edwardian poems to the gaudy tree frog sitting on the limb of a willow tree singing God's psalms in a falsetto voice. The tree, like us, is shedding its summer voice and drifting into dark days that vacillate back and forth between warm and cold, orange and white. The brook is fading into a rivulet as it meets the summer's end, and the aging owl with fading memories heaves a mournful sound at the day's closing, and I, sitting under a barren sycamore tree, bemoan the loss of another summer.

Spring to Be

When the air becomes calm and wintry dreams have passed us by, near a location where, without a qualm, golden memories never seem to die.... Giant diaphanous clouds ascend over the world; streams flow slowly down a hill, pairs of red-tailed hawks circle mightily, calling zealously with their voices shrill.

I marvel at beautiful flowers in the lea, thrill to the songs of birds singing and the guttural voices of frogs croaking stridently with a new sun beaming.

Someday

Someday... I will walk barefoot in
the ocean of memories
       the sand will caress my thoughts

Someday... sea gulls will forage
for my briny dreams in the forgotten
       consequences of rotting kelp

Someday... suddenly, I will remember
that day... then
       I will paint the scene with an artist's
          brush dipped in sand blown metaphors

Someday... I will etch that special picture upon my
fading mind... so I can't forget...

someday.

The Old Surfer and the Seashore

I call you blue, but you with your rushing hair of white,
Summoned by Neptune, could be called eternity... you
Who are calm during the day, terrifying at night.

I call you deep, but you with soft currents at noon,
Cradling sea creatures in shallow tidal pools in the morning,
At night crackling of flames of twisted limbs covers your roar.

At midnight, stars reflected in your face bewilder my senses;
In the early dawn, your fresh and mumbled waves drift
Onto the cold morning sand hugging the ecru shale cliffs.

Yapping gulls awake and struggle with tossed seaweed,
Terns shriek at the thin-legged sandpipers scurrying to
Gather tasty morsels beaching on the sand near the shore.

I gather sea tossed twigs and start a small fire to cook
My hotdog breakfast and heat my leftover black coffee;
The sea birds gather and wait impatiently for tasty remnants.

I sit motionless, painting the scene in my nomadic soul,
Hoping for larger white crested waves to appear so I can
Slice the twisting current with my aged seven-foot board.

The Old Man and the Ocean

… and, the sunlight he heard not, but tasted the salty wind as it curled across the ocean's sandy shore into his memories and around the obscurity of his weary mind.

It was fall; the cold was absorbed in his rusted bones and he sensed an increasing numbness in his weary body.

The ocean's never-ending tide
hurled rushing waves onto the yellow sand with
negligent abandon, causing the shore to listen
to the whispering sounds of sea creatures.

As the day retreated into memories and
the dusk's orange haze
dipped into thoughts of tomorrow,
the old man sat on the lonely beach, longing for just one more day at the ocean's shore.

The Lonely Timber

I am a sea-borne piece
Of twisted timber,
Drifting in the oceans deep,
Floating aimlessly
On dark, trembling waters
Until, one day, the white
Crested waves tossed me onto
A deserted sandy seashore.

No one heard my
Whispering moans
When I merged with brown kelp
Lying buried
In the rippled sand.
No one heard my anguish
When I was burned in a fire
Beside the shale cliffs.

When I became ashes, I was
Swept away by the tide and
Carried carelessly
Out to the sea again; I
Mingled with lost memories and
Seashells adrift in the
Sea's briny mind,
Forever wandering in silence.

Then one day, a young child
Sifting through the yellow sand
Lifted a seashell to his ears
And heard my ashes crying,
Heard my sad voice echoing

The tale of a mighty
Three-masted ship that sunk,
And which was once my home.

The Frog Outside My Window

The lone frog outside my window croaks its somniferous song into my dreaming ears. Its guttural voice unfastens pleasant memories in the locked caches in my mind. How I love to hear that old frog's song in the night as I coast on clouds in my mind's sky.

Ancient Harmonies

Ancient harmonies
Unlock
Melancholy feelings
In my being.
Old songs emanating from
A ghost saxophone played by
Charlie Parker:
Outrageous notes
In distorted chords,
Evocative pianos playing
In 4/5 time,
Surging… black… white...
Flowing
Freely into my soul.
Inharmonious rhythms grumble
In melodic discord,
Creating a soft nostalgia:
Old songs, oceans of
Jazz played by
Long dead musicians
In recital in their tombs
Stream softly
Into my aging mind....

The Silver Celestial Pen

The silver celestial pen,
Its surface gleaming,
Its ceramic handle smooth,
Is raised… then falls.
An enigmatic inky growl emerges,
Forming oblique allegories in the
Desolate earth at dusk.

Peals of thunder
Echo words across the
Heavens:
The pen weaves
An archetype with each
Downward thrust;
The moon
Is pierced…
Golden rays
Seep downward
Onto the damp earth,
Words, metaphors, sentences
Echoing onto ancient ground
Construct bucolic rhymes
Where poets collect them and
Place them inside books.

Sitting in My Orchard

In the orange dust of the
Wintry morning, I sit in the
Orchard where roses are
Feeling their years, as am I:
We are all starting to know
That the time is approaching
Where we will be pruned
And allowed to sleep.

Rain clouds in the distance
Oozing darkness…
Ashen colored memories
Enter, then an eerie silence settles.
Deep within the symbols of sky,
Scarlet colored metaphors
Plunge into my aging sinews,
Causing questions of
Morality to go unanswered.

My old dog Nabby, also
Feeling the years, sits by
My side to get her morning
Petting; she looks at me with
The same understanding of that
Which is nearing… our lives'
End. Both of us aware of that
Which is coming, but still
Holding on tightly to the fading
Years.

The Singing Stops

Two giant majestic pine trees, wooden sentinels of our estate, are gone. I remember fall winds curling up the canyon, singing through them in the brisk evenings. They were our supply of Christmas boughs, vibrant greenery for the mantel, pinecone-laden limbs for the front gates, welcoming holiday visitors and kin.

After four years of drought, they started to become brown, then the pine beetles took over and tolled their death march one hot summer day. We watched with tears in our eyes as they were cut down, leaving wood chips and Spanish lace all over the yard. The entrance to our house is now barren, and the fall winds have started up the canyon again, but there is no singing in the trees.

It's curious how time creates memories, and our minds reminisce about things that are no longer here. The old saltbox house on the hill is still there, but the mother that lived there is gone and there is no singing there, either. In a few years, we, too, will be cut down and our ashes will be buried... then the singing in this house will stop, too.

The Lonesome House

The lonesome house where her
Mother once lived has piles of
Leaves on its shingled roof, and
Decomposed misery on its
Window sills.
Where a happy face
Once looked out
Sparkling windows,
Now darkness spews
Through dusty panes.

Flowers
In broken vases,
Colorless and dead,
Rugs stark and faded;
Ruined brick walks
Once walked upon
With cheerfulness and mirth,
Now covered with weeds,
Broken bricks, and
Faded dreams.

The sound of footsteps, even
The echoes are gone,
As are welcoming lights
In the musty rooms.

Sitting in gray dust and
Solemnity,
The old furniture is molding.
The old house,
Now in mourning, is

Waiting, waiting…
For someone to buy her and
Fill her with gaiety, life, and
Laughter once again.

His Last Rhyme

Images headed inward,
The incessant drone in
His mind weighed down
By shattered rhythms of
An unfinished poem.
His soul,
Heavy… lead-lined… trudged
Ahead to grasp his ego,
Collect scarlet words that fell to
The floor and died,
Gaudy similes rotting
Under his shoeless iambs.

His soul, perishable as newsprint,
Inky as smudges beneath
His scarred, unfaithful pen,
Warped around a sentence
Which he was too tired to carry.
His fear of nocturnal beings
Born of rusted iron and splintered
Ice, which grow in the night below
His broken window, crushed his
Literary assurance. Too fearful to
Carry common metaphors alone
Across the heavy groans of the night, he
Finally escaped into his past and
Breathed his last rhyme.

About the Author

Dr. Piatt's poems have been nominated for Pushcart and Best of Web awards, and his poems were published in The 100 Best Poems Analogies of 2014 and 2015. He has been honored with many awards for his poetry and has been the featured poet in many magazines. He has published over 850 poems in 90 different poetry magazines, anthologies, and poetry books. He was born in Santa Maria, California and graduated from Santa Maria High School. He earned his BS and MA from California State Polytechnic University at San Luis Obispo, and earned his doctorate from BYU. He lives in Santa Ynez, California, just 30 miles from the mountains to the south and 30 miles from the ocean to the west. He has two children, Ann Kathleen, a spiritual/meditation consultant in Santa Maria, and Wallace, an artist in Santa Barbara. He has one grandchild, James Robert Mullen. He has been married to his wife, critic, and muse, Sandy, for 60 years. She has been his inspiration to write poetry.

Previously Published Poems

Oh, to be Young Again (Magic Cat Press)
As I Remember (Westward Quarterly)
Thoughts of Winter (Viral Cat)
The Coming of Winter (Kritya: A Journal of Poetry)
A Wintry Sky (Penwood Review)
An Ocean's Sonnet (Westward Quarterly)
A Sonnet to Spring (Long Story Short)
Thoughts of Home (Word Catalyst Magazine)
Fall's Arriving (Greensilk Journal)
Childhood Memories (Front Porch Review)
An Ebony Reality (Poetry Breakfast)
Now and Then (Apollo's Lyre)
Motion (Long Story Short)
When I Am All Alone (Viral Cat)
City Dreams (Wilderness House Review)
Pain Covers My Fears (My Word Wizard)
Life (Word Catalyst Magazine)
The Stone (Blue Pepper)
Where Are the Years? (Literary Yard)
Another Day (Wilderness House Review)
Absolution (Emerge Literary Journal)
Flowing (Bumble Jacket Miscellany)
Days I Like (Penwood Review)
Someone is Trying to Steal Your Dreams (Tower Journal)
Should Anyone Worry (Autumn Leaves)
Lonely Thoughts (Tower Journal)
Reflections While Lunching in a Garden (Long Story Short)
I Am Weary (Contraposition)
In the Meadow (From the Heart: Anthology)
The Last Voice of Sanity (TreeHouse)
I'm Going to the River... in My Mind (Garbanzo Literary
        Journal)

Love Danced (TreeHouse)
The Old Coyote (Long Story Short)
My Daughter (Long Story Short)
Nighttime (Wilderness House Review)
Autumn (Long Story Short)
Birth of a Rhyme (Homestead Review)
My Father's Ashes (New England Poetry Journal)
Silence *Paisible de Mes Désirs* (Gold Dust Poetry)
Man's Inequities (Red Ochre)
I Dreamt (Global Poetry)
Twilight Time (Autumn Sound)
Waiting For…. (Vox Poetica)
Sounds of Hope (Viral Cat)
Teach Me (Long Story Short)
I Keep Walking (Wilderness House Review)
Help Me (The Tower Journal)
A Voice (Ancient Paths)
A Childhood Place (The Muse: International Poetry Journal)
Country Road (The American Aesthetic)
The Unwritten Song (Cats With Thumbs)
Daffodils (Long Story Short)
A Red Rose (Long Story Short)
Little Colorful Gargoyles (Long Story Short)
My Grandfather (Greensilk Journal)
Fall Memories (Greensilk Journal)
Time for Autumn (Penwood Review)
The Doll (The Screech Owl)
Vanishing Hours (Poetry Magazine.com)
A Day at the Shore (Viral Cat)
Nature's Home (Tower Journal)
In the Wee Hours (Penwood Review)
After the Spring Gales (Literary Yard)
Change (Poetic Diversity)
Another Time… Another Place? (Contemporary Poetry Digest)
A Sense of Spring (Wilderness House Review)
A Song of Spring (Wilderness House Review)
The Orchard Garden (TreeHouse)

The Hours That Guide the Day (The Tower Journal)
Do Not Be Weary (Contemporary Poetry Digest)
My Valentine Love (From the Heart Anthology)
Weep Not, Robin (The Central Pen)
Separation (Long Story Short)
Sleep (The Screech Owl)
Christmas (Long Story Short)
The Album (The Screech Owl)
I Am (Poetic Diversity)
There is Beauty in the World (Front Porch Review)
He Was (On The Rusk)
In The Garden At Dawn (Poetry Magazine.com)
Cry Not, My Love (Peeking Cat Poetry)
Aging (Miller's Pond)
I Am Worn (Offbeat Literature Journal)
Sweet Aromas (Long Story Short)
An Observation (TreeHouse)
A New Morn (Long Story Short)
The Miniscule Speck in the Heavens (Carcinogenic Poetry)
That Time of the Year (Screech Owl)
Madness (Poetry Magazine.com)
Answers (The Papyrus Journal)
His Last Rhyme (The Homestead Review

www.ingramcontent.com/pod-product-compliance
Lightning Source LLC
LaVergne TN
LVHW051402080426
835508LV00022B/2938